AMC guide to
COUNTRY WALKS NEAR NEW YORK

by William G. Scheller

THE APPALACHIAN MOUNTAIN CLUB
BOSTON, MASSACHUSETTS

COUNTRY WALKS NEAR NEW YORK

by William G. Scheller

If you find any errors in the text or maps, please send a letter to the Appalachian Mountain Club (attn: Country Walks Near New York), 5 Joy Street, Boston, Massachusetts 02108. Due to changes in conditions over time, use of information in this book is at the sole risk of the user.

SECOND EDITION

Photos by Paul Mozell and Tom McWilliam

Editorial direction: Aubrey Botsford
Cover photograph: Chris Maynard
Cover design: Hannus Design Associates
Cartography: Bob Holloran (revisions by David Cooper)
Composition: Chansonette Wedemeyer
Production: Renee LeVerrier and Michael Saenz
Printing: McNaughton & Gunn, Inc., Saline, Michigan

ISBN 0-910146-59-4

5 4 3 2 1   86 87 88 89

To Rich Mara,
with whom I could cheerfully hike from here
to Tibet, this book about our native haunts
is dedicated.

FOREWORD

THIS IS A BOOK about the natural and human history of the open lands which surround New York City. It does not include everything there is to know about the area; that would be an impossible goal for any writer to set. Rather, it is an introduction in twenty parts, each of which invites the reader's own participation.

Since this is a book to be carried in the field as well as read at home, it includes practical information about getting from here to there, as well as descriptions of walking routes and the territory they encompass. For consistency's sake, Manhattan is assumed to be the point of departure, although the area map at the beginning of the book will suggest means of auto travel from outlying areas, and a call to any of the major public transportation authorities should settle questions about buses and trains.

Those new to New York and its environs should be aware that there are five major interconnecting public transit networks operating in and around the city. These are: the Metropolitan Transit Authority's subway and bus system (MTA), including Nassau County lines; the Long Island Railroad (LIRR); private bus companies; the state-operated New Jersey Transit bus lines and commuter trains; and the Port Authority Trans-Hudson (PATH) trains that connect Manhattan with Jersey City and Hoboken. Here are the numbers to call for information concerning these transportation facilities. Where applicable, the locations of major terminals appear in square brackets.

Metropolitan Transit Authority (MTA) (New York City subway and buses): 718-330-1234. *(Nassau County buses):* 516-222-1000.

Long Island Railroad (LIRR): 516-222-2100.

Port Authority Bus Terminal (private and public bus companies): 212-564-8484. [Eighth Avenue, Manhattan, between 40th and 41st streets]

Port Authority Trans-Hudson (PATH) (Manhattan to Jersey City and Hoboken): 201-622-6600. [New York terminals at the corner of 33rd Street and Avenue of the Americas (Sixth Avenue) and at the World Trade Center]

New Jersey Transit (commuter trains and buses): 201-762-5100 from New Jersey; 800-772-2222 from New York.

Determining that public transportation serves a certain point is only part of the walker's planning. It won't do to arrive at an outlying destination, spend the day, and then learn that the last bus or train has left. Always ask about service in both directions, and check again if you plan the same walk during a different season. Every effort has been made to provide accurate information in this book, but transit schedules are dependably changeable.

Many of the distances which can be covered in these walks are variable; often, the same area can offer a two-mile stroll or a ten-mile hike. Decide in advance how long you plan to be on the trail, so that you can work out transportation arrangements as well as lunch and clothing requirements. Most people walk at a pace of between two and three miles an hour; since the trips in this book are intended for recreation rather than rigor, the slower rate will most likely apply. Walking in sand or snow takes about twice as long as a walk of the same length on solid ground.

There are cautions throughout the text about hazards that may be encountered, but one or two general bits of advice will be provided here. First, check the weather forecast before you depart. Dress appropriately for the

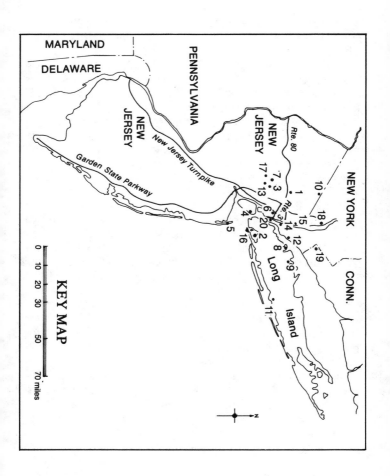

KEY MAP

MARYLAND

DELAWARE

PENNSYLVANIA

NEW JERSEY

NEW JERSEY

NEW YORK

CONN.

Long Island

Garden State Parkway

New Jersey Turnpike

Rte. 80

Rte. 9

7 3
17 1
13
6
20
4 2
16 14
5 8 15
12
9 19
18
10
11

0 10 20 30 50 70 miles

N

weather that you expect to encounter. Wear sturdy, comfortable walking shoes. Be aware that in certain areas there may be human as well as natural hazards, so don't go alone or after dark.

One further admonition — the idea of walking only on a trail may seem to apply only to the pristine backwoods, but a minute's reflection should serve to convince walkers that open lands near large cities are every bit as fragile as the wilderness, and sometimes more so. Heavy use of these places can only be sustained if everyone treats them gently.

I would like to thank everyone who helped with the indoor and outdoor research for this book. My particular appreciation goes to Cathy Barash, Gil Bergen, Mary Cerulli, Stanley Cogan, Jim Dixon, Martin Garille, Holly Hoffman, John Krisko, Mrs. Euphemia Marchitti, Chris Maynard, Jeff Maugans, Julian Miller, John Quinn, Richard Roberts, Mr. and Mrs. William G. Scheller, Sr., Chris Schillizzi, Manny Strumpf, Daniel T. Tompkins, Nick Vallario, and Katy Weidel.

I would also like to thank Paul Mozell and Tom McWilliam for the photographs; David Cooper for his work on the maps of the Hackensack Meadows, Morristown National Historical Park, and Verdrietege Hook; and some of the staff at the Appalachian Mountain Club for their help in putting this book together — Aubrey Botsford for his editing and Renee LeVerrier and Michael Saenz for their production work.

CONTENTS

INTRODUCTION

AFTER SIX WEEKS on the water, a month if you are lucky, you reach a harbor: not a harbor of busy quays and counting houses, of church spires rising against a tangle of hawsers and toiling men, but a wilderness harbor, attended by cormorants and gulls.

To port lies a sandspit dense with scrub pine and holly. Ahead, the bay narrows, its waters hemmed in by low opposing shores that elevate gradually to gentle hills. Both banks of these narrows are themselves parts of islands, but you cannot see that now.

Beyond the narrow place, another bay widens. On both sides the land is broken, marshy, although it rises more perceptibly to starboard, so that its heights command the harbor. Ahead, past several small islands, the wooded prow of another, larger island splits the bay, dividing it into the mouths of two broad rivers. The helmsman holds to port; you enter the wide river. To starboard you see the dark hills and glades of the prow-shaped island, and at glittering intervals streams break the landscape and empty into your river. Is it an island, after all? None of these streams seems to cut it through.

To port, the land begins to rise. The stretch of marsh that reaches back to the far blue hills is suddenly obscured, first by steep, brambly slopes and then by beetling cliffs of dark, pilastered stone. The wall of rock almost distracts you from the point where the starboard island is finally defined, cut clear from the mainland by a channel of water. The big river widens and continues its way through the forest, the lands around it growing higher, truly mountainous.

Godspeed, *Half Moon*. If only we could see what Henry Hudson and his men saw on those days in 1609 — but the view has changed. Behind the prow of that island now stands the helm of the world's commerce, and those with a taste for the natural world argue that this hasn't done the surroundings much good. The point is taken — but the astonishing thing, considering that there are fifteen million people encamped around this harbor, is not how much of nature has been lost, but how much is left. Nearly all of the great natural features discernible to Hudson's sailors, and to the first Europeans to venture inland, are represented in tracts of land which, through chance or enlightened design, have remained essentially undeveloped through the centuries. The holly forest of Sandy Hook, the marshes of Staten Island and Jamaica Bay, the meadows and hills of New Jersey, the heights of the Palisades and upper Manhattan Island — none of these remain entirely as it was, yet none has been altogether lost. Where these places have been touched by settlement, their stories often fascinate even more: the human experience here is older and richer than thirty years of expressways, shopping malls, and hamburger franchises might suggest.

The purpose of this book is twofold: to encourage the discovery of the metropolitan area's remaining natural places, and to remind residents of — and visitors to — New York, New Jersey, and Connecticut of what stands to be lost through neglect, or through a fatalistic attitude toward development. Perhaps you enjoy walks in a favorite country spot of your own, one with a more tenuous claim to preservation than most of the places in this book. Well, keep an eye on it. Don't ever take it for granted.

1

GARRET MOUNTAIN RESERVATION/PATERSON

Walking — 5 to 8 miles, depending on routes chosen. From South Paterson or Paterson train stations, through Paterson, and across the highlands at the summit of Garret Mountain. Basalt cliffs, mixed hardwood forest, museums, a view of the Passaic Valley and Falls, and industrial history.

"**P**ATERSON," WROTE WILLIAM CARLOS WILLIAMS at the beginning of the epic poem to which he gave the city's name, "lies in the valley under the Passaic Falls/its spent waters forming the outline of his back." Applying gender to cities is poetic license: who can argue with that? A topographer, though, might take issue with Williams's identifying the Passaic as Paterson's spine. Its lifeblood, perhaps — but the spine is surely the First Watchung Mountain, called Garret Mountain just south of where it is cloven by the river and its great waterfall. This walk explores the county reservation atop Garret Mountain, with a look at a silk baron's castle and the city which he and thousands of immigrant weavers spun along the valley of the Passaic.

The best approach to Paterson is by rail, and the Conrail commuter trains which run along the old Erie-Lackawanna line stop at two stations convenient to the Garret Mountain walker. The South Paterson train is closer to the reservation, but if you get on or off at the Paterson station, you will have the opportunity to walk through the oldest part of the city on your way to the mountain. The ideal itinerary might be based on arriving at one

station and leaving from the other, depending on whether you prefer bricks in the morning and trees in the afternoon, or vice versa.

PUBLIC TRANSIT: PATH trains run from 33rd Street and the World Trade Center to the Erie-Lackawanna station in Hoboken. From there, take a NJ Transit train down the old Erie Main Line to South Paterson or Paterson, depending on your choice of walking routes. From South Paterson station, walk up Main Street toward St. Joseph's Hospital (large complex of buildings on right) to the corner of Barclay Street, opposite the hospital. Turn left on Barclay, and follow it three blocks to Marshall Street, where it becomes Valley Road. Follow Valley Road over Highway 20; just beyond, on your right, is the entrance road to the reservation. Total distance from the station is less than 1 mile.

From Paterson station, turn left onto Ward Street and continue five blocks to Main Street. Turn left and walk one block to Oliver Street, then right on Oliver and, after one block, left onto Marshall Street. Follow Marshall Street ¾ mile to Valley Road, bear right, and look for the reservation entrance on your right. Total distance from the station is 1.6 miles.

AUTOMOBILE: Take Interstate 80 West to Paterson. Get off at exit marked "Madison Avenue — Clifton." Take Madison Avenue to Main Street. Turn right onto Main, pass St. Joseph's Hospital, and turn left onto Barclay Street (corner opposite hospital). Follow Barclay past Marshall Street, where it becomes Valley Road; look for the Reservation entrance on your right just after you cross over Route 20.

Whether you approach Paterson by train or by car, the dominant feature of your westward view will be Garret Mountain. Al-

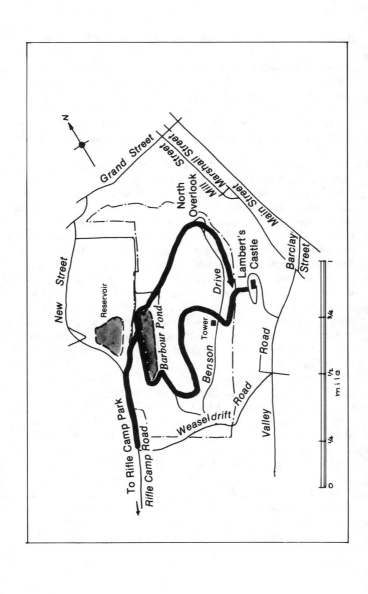

though at less than 600 feet it is hardly more than a hill, the "mountain" clearly commands its surroundings, turning an immense traprock cliff toward the city. This basaltic rock face is volcanic in origin, representing lava flows long concealed beneath layers of sandstone. With the sandstone eroded away, the columnar parapets of hardened lava stand exposed. From the west, though, the Passaic Valley rises to meet the height of the cliffs much less precipitously; a wooded plateau lies atop the wall of basalt.

The Dutch were the earliest of the white settlers in the environs of Paterson. Deeds for farmland in what is now Passaic County were obtained from the Lenni Lenape Indians in 1679. The area's chief Dutch settlement in those days was called Acquackanonk. This was a place well below the falls and to the east of modern-day Paterson. In the Delaware tongue spoken by local Indians, the name meant "place in a rapid stream where fishing is done with a bush net" — this is, a tangle of brush set in the middle of a dam of stones. In 1680, a white man first journeyed upriver to the falls. Within two years, squat Dutch farmhouses began to dot the valley, and their owners' landholdings spread farther west, toward what was then called Wesel Mountain. "Wesel" was a small settlement between the mountain and the river; the name comes from a town on the Dutch-German frontier.

The settlers eventually turned to the forested upland beyond the cliffs as a source of firewood and lumber, and even as an open grazing area for cattle, but white men first made regular forays to Garret Mountain in imitation of an Indian hunting practice. The Lenni Lenape, for whom the pursuit of game was necessarily more a matter of expediency than sport, would herd deer to the edges of the cliffs, and then drive them off to their deaths. Paleontologists tell us that this is one of the most ancient methods of hunting; only three hundred years ago, it fed the families of New Jersey's first European colony as it had countless generations of the Lenni Lenape.

By the time farmers began to till the Passaic Valley, New

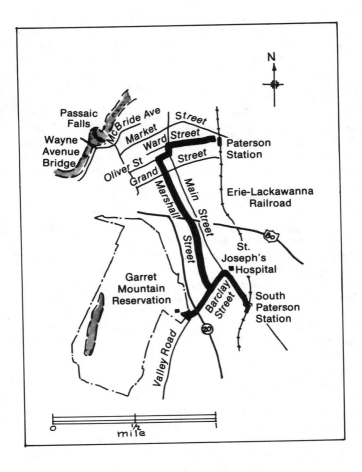

Amsterdam had long since fallen to the British. But Dutch people, culture, and nomenclature were commonplace in the area for well over a century afterwards, and are still a part of North Jersey life. The most durable reminders of the early days are the brownstone, gambrel-roofed farmhouses which survive, like immovable boulders, within the bedroom suburbs of Passaic and Bergen Counties.

Garret Mountain did not get its present name until after 1812. In that year, according to local legend, members of the "Garret Society" — so called because of the group's habit of holding secret meetings in garrets — lugged an artillery piece to the top of Paterson's mountain in the hours before dawn on the Fourth of July, and woke the little city with a bang. The citizens learned who was responsible, and the name of the pranksters' fraternity (so the story goes) stuck to the mountain. Antiquarians with more of a linguistic orientation, however, frown at the cannon story and point out that in the Jersey Dutch patois of the seventeenth century, "Gebarrack" meant "at the mountain," and was corrupted into "Garret." You may take your pick.

After the mountain itself, the first feature that stands out in the landscape west of Main Street and Route 80 is a brownstone mansion and, above it on the cliff, a crenellated tower. The mansion is Lambert's Castle, built for Catholina Lambert, a Scottish-born silk manufacturer, in 1892. Four years later, Lambert raised his 70-foot tower for use as an observatory and summer house.

Lambert's story is a common parable of the Gilded Age — a poor immigrant ascends in business, builds his stately home (Lambert called his castle "Belle Vista"), and sets about collecting art and entertaining the great and powerful. Silk built Paterson, and it made Catholina Lambert; his breakfast room was hung with Monets and Renoirs, and a reception for President McKinley was the highlight of the 1898 social season. Even though troubles in the silk business forced the sale of some paintings in 1914, Lambert held on to his boyhood dream until his death in 1923 at the age of 88. In 1928, the Passaic County Park System acquired the property and 575 adjacent acres, and the Garret Mountain Reservation came into being. In addition to serving as headquarters of both the Park System and the Passaic County Historical Society, the castle houses a randomly eclectic but interesting museum in which local historical artifacts predominate. The tower has not proven so useful; its entrance is sealed off, and its foundations offer a record of who loves whom in the Paterson *demimonde*. Still, it seems indestructible, like an upthrust bastion of the cliffs themselves.

THE WALK: A short hike along the looping entrance road of the reservation will bring you to Lambert's Castle. From the parking lot at the rear of the castle, follow the paved path uphill to where the stone steps begin. Climb the steps, noting the traprock formations; at the top, turn right and follow the path through a sharp switchback and on to the tower, where there is an excellent view of Passaic and Bergen Counties all the way to the George Washington Bridge. Facing the tower in the direction from which you approached, turn right and follow the path across a park road and the trail that parallels it. At this point the path becomes indistinct, but you can head straight through the woods until you reach a picnic area. Just short of the picnic area, turn left onto a bridle trail. Turn left onto this trail. After another ⅓ mile, turn right at a trail intersection and cross a park road. You will next pass a small picnic and parking area; Barbour Pond is just ahead. The walk along the mossy traprock rim on the west bank of the pond is pleasant, and — if you are licensed and equipped — you can fish for the pond's stocked trout.

From Barbour Pond, there are several alternatives to returning by the same route that you took from the castle. If you have the time and don't mind the extra mileage, a walk from the southern end of the pond will bring you to Rifle Camp Park, where there are bird blinds, a forestry trail, a geology study area, and — at the park's nature center — a working seismograph.

BARBOUR POND TO RIFLE CAMP PARK: On the opposite side of Barbour Pond (see map), a path bears right toward Rifle Camp Road. Turn left onto Rifle Camp Road and walk 3/5 of a mile; the park entrance is on the left. Along the way, stop at Bromilow's (on the right) for homemade chocolates. The nature center is 4/5 of a mile past the park entrance.

If you stay within the Reservation and head north from Barbour Pond, you can enjoy a magnificent view of Paterson, the Passaic River Valley, and — if the day is clear — all of the lands between the Ramapo Mountains and New York harbor. A look at the city below North Lookout will help give you some idea of which areas you might like to explore should you opt for a Paterson walk on the way back to the train station.

TO NORTH LOOKOUT: From the north end of Barbour Pond (opposite the old pavilion) follow the auto road or either of the trails paralleling it until you reach a meadow and the lookout. From the tower, turn right onto the auto road or parallel trails (rather than crossing the road and heading toward the pond) and continue along the top of the cliff toward the lookout. If you have approached the lookout from the pond, return to the tower via the cliff-top path.

Now you are looking down upon the first planned manufacturing city in the United States. Stand at the northwest end of the lookout's stone guardrail and focus on a stadium in the middle distance. Let your eye travel slightly to the left, and you will see the reason for the city's old industrial prominence: the Great Falls of the Passaic, an 80-foot chasm second only to Niagara in the eastern U.S. Alexander Hamilton visited these falls in the years just after the Revolution, and, having advised President Washington of their potential, founded the Society for the Establishment of Useful Manufactures here in 1791. The city, before then a patchwork of Dutch farms and villages, was incorporated at the same time.

By the mid-nineteenth century, Paterson was on its way to becoming the "Silk City," although locomotive works were also important. And it was here, in one of the brick mills that still stand amidst a network of now-stagnant raceways, that Samuel Colt engaged in a radical new venture: the manufacture of his first revolvers.

Many of the mills stand empty or half-occupied now, and Paterson is not the city that it was. A disastrous fire in 1902, labor turbulence in the early part of this century, and the advent of synthetic textiles all took their toll. But the city, as it remains, is a vast and poignant museum of the industrial revolution in America.

TO THE FALLS AND OLD INDUSTRIAL DISTRICT: If you are heading to or from Paterson station, turn onto Main Street and then left onto Market Street (see map). Follow Market Street three blocks to its end, passing an outdoor exhibit of locally built steam locomotives and the Paterson Museum, located in an adjacent mill building. Then turn right and walk uphill two blocks to the Wayne Avenue Bridge. The small park to the right of the bridge offers a fine view of the falls. Just before you cross the Wayne Avenue Bridge, turn right for the footbridge across the chasm. Suspended above the falls, you will feel the spray and the power of the cataract, and come to understand what moved Hamilton to conceive this city of "useful manufactures."

2

JAMAICA BAY

Walking — 6 miles, all trails; add 2 miles if walking to and from subway station. Wildlife refuge within the boundaries of greater New York, set amidst salt marsh and freshwater ponds at the center of the islands in Jamaica Bay.

"**I**T IS LIKEWISE VOTED and agreede upon by the Towne that whosoever will take the pains for to destroy the wolves either by diging of pits to catche them in or by shooteing shall for every wolfe soe kilde theire heds being brought to the Towne and nailed upon a tre shall have for every wolfe 7 bushels of indean corne."

—from the proceedings of the town meeting,
Jamaica, New York, February 6, 1663.

There are no wolves around Jamaica Bay today; everyone collected their indean corne and went home to make mush. But in many respects, the bay and the marshlands that surround it have changed less in 300 years than have spelling and syntax in the English language. It is remarkable enough to be able to stand on the shores of a clean freshwater pond, surrounded by the labyrinthine channels of a salt water archipelago, and watch egrets take wing against an open vista framed by Kennedy Airport and the skyline of Manhattan. But even more miraculous is Jamaica Bay's survival of a close brush with ruin early in this century.

Times of prosperity beget schemes for even greater gain. So it was in 1905, when Edward M. Grout, New York City comptroller, addressed a "communication" to the commissioners of the

city's Sinking Fund. His concern was with a shortage of developable harbor space within the city, and the loss of business which this might cause New York — particularly in light of the "strong inducements offered by land syndicates in New Jersey." The more things change. . . .

Grout's attention focused on Jamaica Bay. "There is here a vast territory of unimproved land, of land under water," he wrote the commissioners. "Little or nothing has been done to reclaim what is practically waste land and water, and in consequence its present value is insignificant. . . . My proposition is that the City should at once take up . . . a comprehensive scheme for the full development of this property." He went on to suggest "reclaiming the salt marshes, filling in the shallow parts and hummocks of the bay, bulkheading the islands and shores throughout their entire extent, and opening up such channels . . . as may best develop the locality for its future needs and opportunities. . . . It is possible I believe thus to furnish here a centering point for great manufacturing interests, which will subsequently produce a large and ever-increasing revenue to the City of New York." Grout saw 20 square miles of developable land around Jamaica Bay, and stressed that new rail links with New York and the mainland would make the area an unparalleled harbor location. He even knew where the necessary landfill would come from — his proposal suggested both Brooklyn garbage and the soil turned up in subway excavations. Jamaica Bay, the comptroller proclaimed, "may be made either a commercial or manufacturing Venice, or a Venice of homes, or both."

Grout's plan did not take off, but neither did it die. In 1922, the city committed itself to the replacement of the scattered marshlands of Jamaica Bay with two large islands, to be approached by a series of navigation canals, and to be bordered with miles of industrial wharves. The resulting harbor, boosters claimed, would be greater than those of Liverpool, Hamburg, and Rotterdam combined. Work never began, but the proposed superport still appeared on city planning maps as late as 1938. In

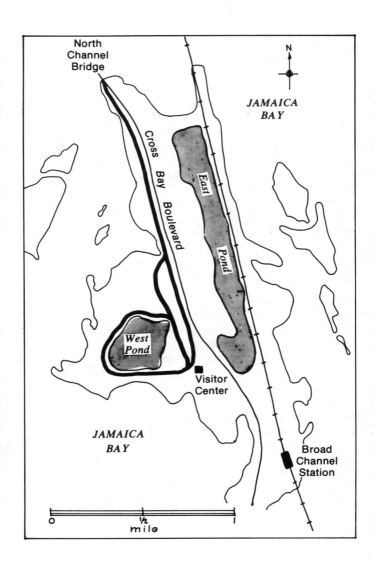

North Channel
Bridge

*JAMAICA
BAY*

Cross Bay Boulevard

*East
Pond*

*West
Pond*

Visitor
Center

*JAMAICA
BAY*

Broad
Channel
Station

0   ½   1
mile

that year, New York City Parks Commissioner Robert Moses sent a letter to Mayor Fiorello LaGuardia, in which he noted that Jamaica Bay "is the only large remaining area in New York City whose character is undetermined," and urged final scrapping of the harbor/industrial plan. Moses proposed the building of new sewage treatment plants, so that the bay's waters would become suitable for swimming, and the transferral of all islands in the area to the Parks Department. "Must we continue the construction of expensive, artificial swimming pools in this region," Moses wrote, "where the waters of Jamaica Bay, protected from pollution, can meet the problem as nature intended it to be met?"

Moses won out; the vast deepwater port became a paper curiosity. And though his hopes for public bathing have yet to be realized, the progression of attitudes regarding the potential of Jamaica Bay is a reflection of awakening environmental consciousness in our time. First, it was viewed as a waste to be reclaimed, and next as a recreational resource for the people. In 1953, the Jamaica Bay Wildlife Refuge was created out of 9,170 of the bay's 14,000 acres of land and water. Finally, in 1973, the federal government consolidated the preserve and adjacent bay shores into the new Gateway National Recreation Area, in response to the needs of both man and wildlife.

Gateway was the first project of its kind in the United States. Previous national park acquisitions had been made in places remote from civilization and difficult of access to most of the population. As the 1970s began, legislators and park officials came to realize that urban dwellers too needed open spaces, and saw that a unique opportunity existed for the establishment of a major national park in the heart of our most congested metropolitan area. Gateway's component parts were there for the asking; nearly all were already in the hands of either the federal government or the states of New York and New Jersey. Some had served military purposes, and some had long been parks. In many ways, the Jamaica Bay Wildlife Refuge was the jewel among the diffuse parcels of land which were assembled to create the 26,000-acre recreation area.

The name "Gateway" occurred to the park's proponents early in its planning. The twin arms of Sandy Hook, in New Jersey, and Breezy Point, on Brooklyn's Rockaway peninsula, are indeed the portals of the New World. They greeted not only Hudson and Verrazano, but millions of other voyagers who passed through the Narrows, looked with hope and apprehension into the canyons that commence at the Battery, and disembarked at a little depot off the shore of Jersey City. Plymouth Rock is a fine symbol, but Ellis Island is a fact.

Gateway National Recreation Area became a fact by an act of the 92nd Congress, late in 1972. It was put together from federal, state, and municipal lands on Staten Island, Sandy Hook, and Jamaica Bay. The latter area presented one of the greatest challenges to the park's developers; the legislation that created Gateway specifically requires that the Secretary of the Interior "shall administer and protect the islands and waters within the Jamaica Bay Unit with the primary aim of conserving the natural resources, fish, and wildlife located therein and shall permit no development or use of the area which is incompatible with this purpose." Thus the old wildlife refuge remains essentially that — a refuge, where human visitors are welcome but management programs first address the well-being of the wetlands ecosystem. Permits, though easily obtained at the unit's visitor center, are nonetheless required, and automobile parking spaces are kept to a minimum. Boating is also by permit only; canoes are an exception, but permission is required if canoeists intend to beach on any of the dozens of islands in the bay. Many of these islands — some mere hummocks, which contract and expand with the tides — are nesting grounds for some of the 322 bird species spotted within the area.

PUBLIC TRANSIT: Take the IND A (8th Avenue Express) or CC (8th Avenue Local) to Broad Channel station. From here, head west (right side of tracks as you approach station) to Cross Bay Boulevard; cross to boulevard and walk north (right) to the visitor center (approximately 0.9 mile from station). Or, take the IRT No. 2 (7th Avenue Express) to New Lots Avenue, Brooklyn; from here, the Q21A bus runs to the visitor center.

AUTOMOBILE: Take the Belt Parkway to Cross Bay Boulevard, then drive south (toward Rockaway) to the visitor center. The entrance is exactly 1½ miles south of North Channel Bridge.

THE WALK: The Gateway Jamaica Bay Unit Visitor Center is located at the very center of the wildlife refuge, at the point where several recommended walks begin. The first of these circles West Pond, one of two man-made freshwater enclosures in the refuge. The water level of the pond is carefully controlled, so that a shoreline mudflat is provided for waterfowl during Atlantic flyway migration times. Park naturalists also periodically add fresh water to the pond, and remove algae from its shores — the purpose being to interrupt the botulism cycle which affects migratory birds. Despite these adjustments, West Pond appears completely natural and affords fine birding opportunities. (West Pond circuit approximately 1¾ miles.)

The North Spur Walk, which also begins at the visitor center, extends through the "upland" area of the refuge, where a sandy-soil forest of forage-producing plant species was started in 1953. A booklet describing the numbered tree and shrub specimens to be seen along this trail is available at the center. (North Spur Trail approximately ¾ mile.)

The longest of the refuge walks (no paths exist in the marshlands on the opposite side of Cross Bay Boulevard) extends for about 1¾ miles in a northerly direction, ending at the North Channel Bridge. This route branches off from

*the North Spur Trail, leaves the upland forest, and parallels
the western shore of the bay. Despite lingering evidence of
less gentle treatment of the salt marsh — broken piers,
twisted fragments of old railroad tracks, an occasional
automobile tire — the walk to the bridge offers a good view
of the islands in the bay, a sense of the area's location in
relation to more familiar metropolitan sights, and still
another chance to observe wading, shore, and marsh birds
as well as the seasonal formations of ducks and geese. At
the bridge, you'll find fishermen casting for flounder, cod,
striped bass, and bluefish, the fortunes of which will be a
sure indication of whether Robert Moses' hopes for Jamaica
Bay's water quality will ultimately be realized.*

3

SOUTH MOUNTAIN RESERVATION

Walking and ski-touring — 5 miles. A look at a historic train station, followed by a walk through forest glades and along the crest of South Mountain, in one of the oldest public reservations of its kind.

LIKE SOME OF THE OTHER trips in this book, this excursion to the South Mountain Reservation in Essex County, New Jersey begins at the old Erie-Lackawanna terminal in Hoboken. Now serving as the point of arrival and departure for Conrail commuter trains, this grand, copper-clad enclosure dates back far beyond the merger of the Erie and Lackawanna roads, to the days when the Delaware, Lackawanna, and Western was a legend on the high iron. This was a railroad that painted the sides of its rails with black enamel at station platforms; this was a railroad that kept its own gardens, so that there would always be fresh flowers for its dining car tables. This was a railroad — and when it came time to build a main terminal, the DL&W approached the task the way Cunard or White Star would have gone about launching a flagship. It simply had to be the best.

Construction of the terminal began in the spring of 1906. The line had had station fires in the past, so the directors insisted on a fireproof structure. Building materials were thus limited to concrete, copper, wrought iron, steel, stone, and glass, and even the furnishings of the ticket office were made of metal. Limestone and bronze were used lavishly in the main waiting room, which measured 90 by 100 feet. The lofty ceiling of this room is typical of the terminals of the period, but a departure

from convention was made in the design of the train sheds. The fourteen tracks are not enclosed under an expansive vaulted arch, but instead are housed beneath a low, continuous series of individual sheds that are architecturally distinct though interconnected and open to each other. The effect is of a shed for each track, with rows of cast iron columns supporting the whole. During the rare times when the 607-foot sheds are empty or nearly empty of trains, the columns are visible throughout, and cut the space below the vast roof into vertical bars of grey light. The last, high-numbered tracks below the shed are used for ordinary commuter runs now, but it was from here that the crack long-distance trains used to leave for the cities of the midwest. The symbol of the Chicago limited was a lady in a snowy cloak, worn as proof of the clean-burning qualities of hard coal:

> My coat stays white
> Both day and night
> Along the road of anthracite.

The name of the lady, and the train, was Phoebe Snow.

The DL&W ran ferries as well as trains, and the new terminal was intended to impress passengers arriving from across the Hudson, as well as those coming in from the suburbs by rail. Six barrel-vaulted ferry slips, their roofs sheathed in copper like the rest of the building, dominated 600 feet of river frontage; commuters could board the boats at two levels of the great concourse. The concourse itself contained a restaurant with a river-facing balcony, a barbershop, and an emergency hospital. There was to be no trouble in discerning the slips from lower Manhattan; according to company promotional literature of the time, "at night . . . they will be brilliantly illuminated. It is the intention of the officers of the Lackawanna to make the Hoboken Terminal the most conspicuous place on the Hudson." Those were not the days of the low profile.

But our object is to put this verdigris-covered temple behind us, and to chug out to the South Mountain Reservation in

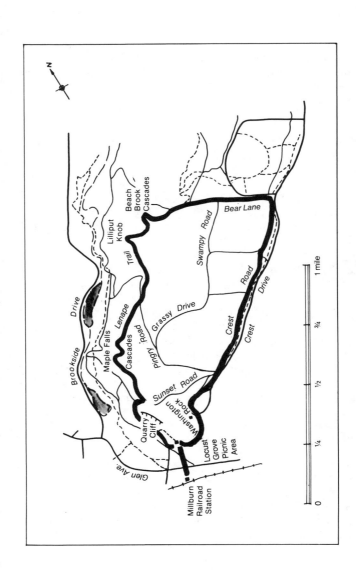

Millburn. Perhaps "whirr" would be a better word; the lines to this part of Jersey are electrified. They've been that way since the early 1930s, when Thomas Edison himself inaugurated the new service, and until a few years ago the original rolling stock was in use. The new cars are a bit more reliable, if less picturesque.

PUBLIC TRANSIT: Take the PATH trains from either 33rd Street or the World Trade Center (the ferries are no more) to the Conrail (NJ Transit) terminal in Hoboken; there, board the train for Millburn. When you get off the train, walk across the parking lot to Glen Avenue, which is on your right as you are coming from Hoboken. Almost directly across from the station is the Locust Grove entrance to the South Mountain Reservation.

AUTOMOBILE: Take the Holland Tunnel to Interstate 78, the New Jersey Turnpike Extension. When you reach Newark, stay on Interstate 78 west, continuing past the Turnpike south exit (don't get on the Turnpike south) for about 8 miles to the Vaux Hall Road (Millburn) exit. Take Vaux Hall Road north to Millburn Avenue, and turn left (west). Continue west after road changes to one-way on Essex Street. Turn right at Lackawanna Place (railroad station). Across Glen Avenue is the Locust Grove parking lot. (An automobile will also give you access to other parts of this extensive reservation; maps are available at the park police station on South Orange Avenue [Route 510], which bisects the reservation.)

The South Mountain Reservation is the largest parcel of park land in what is the nation's oldest county park system. It occupies parts of the crests and foothills of both the First and Second Watchung Mountains (see Chapter 13), and has largely been maintained as a near-wilderness. This is no mean feat, considering the fact that Essex is New Jersey's most populous county. It is instructive to look into the history of the Essex County Park Commission, which was only recently dissolved as part of a county reorganization plan, and into its early attempts to preserve South Mountain.

The idea of municipal parks grew with the industrialization and urbanization of the nineteenth century. When population centers were small, and open countryside was accessible to pedestrian townspeople, there was little thought of setting aside land against a time when it might be needed for aesthetic and recreational purposes. The New England town commons might be considered an exception; but, they were originally communally held grazing lands, not picnic groves or playing fields. As cities such as Newark grew, however, farsighted citizens realized that industry and block development would soon absorb all of the open land available to evening strollers and working people on weekend outings. The idea had first been a European one; now, its time had come in the United States.

After a quarter century of alternating proposals, disagreements, and lethargy, the city fathers of Newark and the Oranges finally agreed, in April of 1894, to submit draft enabling legislation for an Essex County park system to the New Jersey state legislature. The legislation was approved, and a temporary commission began to consider park locations, one of which had been strongly suggested early in 1894 by an editorial writer for the Newark *Sunday Call:*

> There is available for public park purposes at moderate expense the finest park site known near any Eastern city — the slope and crown of Orange (South) Mountain. Delay will remove it from possible use as a park, for it is being rapidly occupied by residences.

By the spring of 1895, a permanent Park Commission had been named, and its members immediately set about requisitioning funds for study and land acquisition. A landscape architect and engineer were hired. One of the charges to these professionals was to recommend areas to be purchased for a large reservation in the Oranges; the expediency with which this study was begun indicates the seriousness with which the commissioners took the *Call*'s concern over residential encroachment on South Mountain. Actual purchase and capital improvement of the lands that became South Mountain Reservation had begun by the end of 1895.

Acquisition of property for the reservation was made over a period of 41 years, until the present 2,048 acres had been set aside. This figure represents nearly half of the acreage currently held by the Essex County Department of Parks, Recreation, and Cultural Affairs, which is the successor to the original five-member commission.

The "slope and crown of Orange Mountain" have proven their worth as a county reservation, despite early worries that they might actually be too far from populated areas. Today, of course, the towns of South Orange, Maplewood, and Millburn press right against the reservation's borders, and transportation is no problem. But the wisdom of having left so much of it virtually untouched is apparent as soon as the walker leaves Millburn station behind — South Mountain is one of the few places left this close to New York that offers a sense of the "Jersey primeval" which settlers saw as they pushed westward from the Hudson. Its backbone is basalt, thrust upwards through layers of sandstone and shale. Evidence of glaciation abounds in the form of boulders and smaller rock debris which mark the ice sheet's terminal moraine, and in the close undulation of carved-out valleys that make some trails seem like anything but tame paths in a county park. The forest is primarily mixed hardwood, mostly high-crowned oaks and maples, with tall hemlocks and a variety of smaller successional species providing contrast. Although much of this land was no doubt cut over at one time — even though too steep to farm, it could have afforded pasture — it is not hard to imagine that there are sections that have always been strangers to the axe, where an unbroken plant succession dates back to the last ice age.

SOUTH MOUNTAIN RESERVATION

THE WALK: What follows is one of many South Mountain walks. Remember, the reservation stretches far to the north of the territory covered here, and other possibilities — such as a trip to the Turtle Back Zoo — offer themselves if you drive or travel by bus through the Oranges instead of taking the train to Millburn. But this southern portion of the reservation offers a wonderfully varied sampling of South Mountain's terrain and views.

Just uphill, to the right of the Locust Grove parking area, is a small picnic grove. Walk through the picnic grove toward where a narrow trail leads uphill (far corner of grove, diagonally opposite parking area). Wherever the trail appears to fork, bear to the left. This will take you away from the houses on the edge of the reservation. After the second fork you will be following a fairly well-defined uphill trail (notice white blazes on several trees). When you reach a thicket, bear right. It is likely there will be a few deadfalls along the way, so be prepared to go over or under. Follow this trail until it reaches a low stone wall, which encircles a small grassy field, and bear left to reach the higher stone wall that borders paved Crest Drive and the Washington Rock overlook. Turn left to reach Washington Rock.

As on Garret Mountain and other points along the Watchung range, there is considerable pitch to the slope that leads to South Mountain's eastern crest. The views here are fine, particularly at the southern extreme of the reservation. Washington Rock is so named because, according to tradition, the commander-in-chief stood here and watched his troops hold off the British in a campaign that resulted in the enemy's final departure from New Jersey. The British had been trying to reach high ground and cut through to the rebel stores at Morristown. During their retreat, they burnt the villages of Union and Springfield.

When you look out from the same promontory today, it is hard to imagine how General Washington could have stood there and followed the course of battles many miles distant. But ours is a much more heavily forested landscape — even the densely populated suburbs below South Mountain are so thick with trees that only the highways, shopping malls, and large public buildings stand out during summer and early fall. In revolutionary times, the lowlands east to New York Harbor were mostly under till, and a man with a spyglass could survey the movement of troops across three counties from atop this rock.

Looking toward the southeast horizon from Washington Rock, you can see the hills of Staten Island; beyond them, the Verrazano Bridge rises nearly 700 feet above the Narrows. In the middle distance are the great refineries of Linden and Carteret, while directly below are spread the Union County suburbs. Turning due east — to the left — you are in line with the towers of downtown Newark and their giant shadows in lower Manhattan. To the north the Watchung Range continues, toward Paterson and the Passaic River Valley. And not a British regular in sight.

From Washington Rock, turn right and follow the unpaved Crest Road, a trail that runs inside and to the left of Crest Drive. Continue until you reach a parking area (about 1 mile) at which a paved road meets Crest Drive. Turn left and continue until the paved road bears right at the end of the parking area; from here, continue straight ahead along unpaved Bear Lane. Continue, passing a path intersection at the left, to reach a T-intersection about ¼ mile from the parking area. Turn left here, heading downhill, and begin looking for the point, about 500 feet from the T-intersection, where the Lenape Trail crosses the lane. This trail is narrow and can be tricky to locate, so look hard. Turn left onto the trail, and keep an eye out for yellow blazes on the trees.

SOUTH MOUNTAIN RESERVATION

From here, the Lenape Trail crosses the Beech Brook Cascades and passes Lilliput Knob. It crosses the unpaved Pingry Road and heads toward Maple Falls Cascades, which offer a fine example of a glacially carved traprock formation. Finally, the trail reaches Sunset Road (little more than an unpaved trail itself); if you reach a fence at the top of an old quarry cliff you've gone too far. Turn right (downhill) on Sunset Road, turn left at the fork, and descend to the Locust Grove parking area.

Although South Mountain Reservation is the crowning achievement of the old Essex County Park Commission, it is by no means the county's only natural attraction. On other forays west of Newark you may wish to visit Eagle Rock Reservation (just south of Montclair) or the Mills Reservation, between Cedar Grove and Upper Montclair, where the rolling hills are ideal for cross-country skiing. The Essex County Parks Department also maintains a Center for Environmental Studies on Eagle Rock Avenue in Roseland (unfortunately, not accessible by public transportation), which offers a series of seasonal educational programs as well as walks in adjacent undeveloped parkland along the upper reaches of the Passaic River. The Center is also a good place to launch a canoe for an exploration of nearby Great Piece Meadow, a pocket wilderness through which the Passaic quietly snakes.

4

STATEN ISLAND

A visit to New York City's least-known borough, where a former city park and a decommissioned military facility have been incorporated into the Gateway National Recreation Area. At Great Kills Park, walk through a dense "forest" of phragmites toward a sandspit overlooking Lower New York Bay.

"**W**E'LL TAKE MANHATTAN, the Bronx and Staten Island too. . . ." Even in song, the borough of Richmond comes across as an afterthought. It became part of greater New York at the same time as Brooklyn, in 1898, but for many years it was the least accessible part of the city. Until 1928, no bridges connected Staten Island either with the mainland or with the other islands that comprise New York. By 1931, three new spans — the Bayonne and Goethals Bridges and the Outerbridge Crossing — linked Richmond with New Jersey, but it was not until the completion of the Verrazano-Narrows Bridge in 1964 that direct access to Brooklyn and the rest of Long Island was provided. To this day, the only way to travel directly from Manhattan to Staten Island is to take the celebrated ferry, an institution that many New Yorkers rank with the Empire State Building and Central Park among the town's time-proof fixtures.

It's easy, then, to see why Staten Island has long assumed the character of *terra incognita* for even those Jerseyans and New Yorkers who see its low hills each day from across the water. But anyone who enjoys the idea of such a mysterious, half-settled anomaly surviving so close to Times Square had better

think twice: Staten Island is changing faster than almost any part of the metropolitan area. If you make your living developing shopping malls, this will please you immensely — but if you are a country walker, you will be thankful that open spaces such as those now administered by Gateway National Recreation Area have been preserved. You'll also want to take a look around the rest of the island before even more of its landscape is lost.

It is a popular notion that the Verrazano Bridge has been responsible for the Staten Island housing boom. Surely, the massively elegant 2½-mile span has made "a place in the suburbs" available even to commuters who wish to remain in the city proper. But the bridge is only an instrument serving a shifting population; other such instruments are the townhouse apartment tract and the garden condominium. People need homes, but one wishes that these amber waves of plywood wouldn't spread so blindly and relentlessly, making Staten Island seem like nothing so much as a housing development proving ground for New Jersey.

But open lands remain, and they represent a varied sampling of the island's topography. The Staten Island that we see today is a creature of the last great period of glaciation, as well as of far earlier rock-forming epochs in the earth's history. The base rock here is serpentine, but the material visible on the surface is more likely to consist of random debris carried from New England by the glacier. The heaps of rock and soil that mark the end of the ice sheet's southward movement are called *moraines*; the Harbor Hill Moraine, along with occasional outcrops of base serpentine, is what defines the crest of Staten Island's uplands. These extend roughly along a northeast-southwest line near the center of the island. Todt Hill, just south of the Castleton Corners neighborhood, is the highest point on the ridge; in fact, its 410-foot elevation makes it the loftiest spot on the North American coast south of Maine's Cadillac Mountain.

Southeast of this line of hills, Staten Island's terrain is composed of the finer glacial debris known as "outwash." This area, of course, has always been more vulnerable to the land-

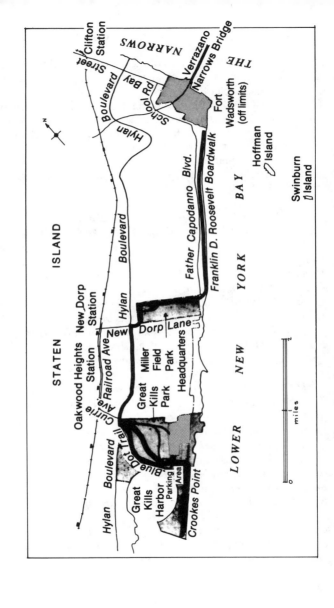

building and -subtracting forces of the open ocean. (For a more detailed discussion of the influence of glaciation on modern landforms, see Chapter 8.)

Our Staten Island walk lies to the south, along the glacial outwash plain and barrier beaches that face Lower New York Bay. Much of this shoreland has been gathered into the 26,000-acre Gateway National Recreation Area (see Chapter 2), the Staten Island headquarters of which are at Miller Field, formerly a military airfield. Gateway's other principal island holding is Great Kills Park.

PUBLIC TRANSIT: Take the Staten Island Ferry from Manhattan. To Miller Field: From ferry, take Staten Island Rapid Transit to New Dorp station, then bus No. 117 down New Dorp Lane to the Field. Or get off at Oakwood Heights station and take bus No. 111 to corner of Hylan Boulevard and New Dorp Lane; walk from here to field entrance. To Great Kills Park: Staten Island Rapid Transit to Oakwood Heights station. Walk south four blocks on Railroad Avenue; then turn left on Currie Avenue and continue to Hylan Boulevard and park entrance. A shuttle bus runs from the entrance to the beach during the summer.

AUTOMOBILE: To Fort Wadsworth/Miller Field: Take Verrazano-Narrows Bridge to Staten Island; get off at Bay Street exit, follow School Road to Bay Street, and turn right. Parking for the fort grounds is at the end of Bay Street. If you wish to drive directly to Miller Field, take the Hylan Boulevard exit after crossing the Verrazano Bridge, and follow Hylan Boulevard south. After approximately three miles, turn left onto New Dorp Lane, which parallels Miller Field. The entrance to the field parking lot is about ¾ mile farther on your left. To Great Kills Park: Proceed as above, but do not turn at New Dorp Lane. Instead, continue on Hylan Boulevard for another two miles. You will see the Gateway entrance sign on your left.

STATEN ISLAND

THE WALK: As of this writing, the city is making repairs to the Franklin D. Roosevelt Boardwalk, which parallels the Lower Bay along South and Midland Beaches for 2¼ miles and makes for a pleasant walk parallel to Father Capodanno Boulevard between off-limits Fort Wadsworth and Miller Field (the location of park headquarters). It may be necessary to detour around construction. (From the boardwalk, you will see two islands about a mile out in the bay. These are Hoffman and Swinburne Islands. These are also part of Gateway, although they are without regular means of access or developed facilities.) Miller Field itself has been developed more as a site for organized recreation than for walking (there are tennis courts, baseball, football, and soccer fields, and a roller hockey rink); however, a pleasant and little-used trail meanders through a swamp oak forest at the field's northwest corner.

The largest and least developed of the Gateway lands on Staten Island is Great Kills Park, a former city facility that encompasses a vast wilderness of phragmites, a shifting sandspit, and the circular enclosure of Great Kills Harbor. It would be good if we could report that Great Kills is accessible from Miller Field (and, ultimately, from Fort Wadsworth), but it simply isn't so: while the walker can make his or her way along the beach for several hundred yards south of the field, access to Great Kills is blocked by the Oakwood Beach Sewage Treatment Plant. The plant is not an intolerable aesthetic intrusion; in fact, park officials and those who have received special permits report excellent birding within its grounds. Nevertheless, it does block the way, so you will have to resort to Hylan Boulevard and the main Great Kills entrance gate.

THE WALK: The best means of making your way through Great Kills Park (and of seeing the most of its animal and plant communities) is to follow the Blue Dot Trail, which begins near the Hylan Boulevard entrance to the park at a

*sign which says "Gateway Equestrian Trail" (right side of
entrance road; several parking spaces available here). You
won't be sharing the trail with horses — the well-marked
foot path quickly departs from the equestrian route, courses
through woodlands, and plunges into what could only be
described as phragmite-sided valleys.*

The tenacity and vigor of phragmites, many of which easily
surpass ten feet in height, can best be appreciated in surroundings (literally, *surroundings*) such as this. Although the fea-
thery-topped weeds enjoy no popularity with naturalists as a
source of bird food, they are ideal cover for pheasant — and it is
a rare day at Great Kills when a Blue Dot Trail walker is not
startled by the resonant "whrrr" and blurred, near-vertical
ascent of the equally surprised birds. Mourning doves, too,
seem to favor the protection which phragmites offer.

*Near the halfway point on the Blue Dot Trail (total trail
length is approximately 2½ miles) you will come upon a
parking area and administration building. (If you have
come by bus or on foot from Miller Field, you may wish to
turn away from the trail here and follow the road that heads
south along the beach toward Crookes Point. Otherwise,
finish the Blue Dot Trail and drive to this main parking
area.) The recommended approach to the point is along the
beach near the bulkhead; the dunes between the harbor and
the bay should not be traversed unless the walker has
received a permit from Gateway headquarters. Birders
may receive such permission; inquire at Miller Field.*

Crookes Point was not always a point — at least, not all day,
every day. Prior to the landfill operations that created the harbor
in the 1940s, the end of this spit was an island at high tide. It was
called Plum Island, after the beach plums which grew there.
Today, the currents of the Lower Bay are doing some engineer-

ing of their own: sand from the point's eastern flank is being washed southward, where it is rounding and widening the tip of the spit. If this process were not to be impeded, the end result would likely be the closing of the harbor channel and, perhaps, an eventual meeting of Crookes Point with the Staten Island mainland. Dredgers will no doubt intervene. But in New York Harbor, there is nothing new about the tug of war between natural forces and those who followed, and still follow, Hudson and Verrazano.

5

SANDY HOOK

Walking — 2 to 5 miles, depending on trails taken; more if a walking trip to Fort Hancock is included. A look at a changing New Jersey barrier beach harboring several interesting plant communities; also a lighthouse and historic fort.

HERE IS WHERE THE Jersey shore begins. The Jersey shore — what conflicting images those two words bring to mind! For over a hundred miles, with few interruptions, stretches one of the finest white sand beaches in the world. Dunes, windswept barrier formations, salt marshes at the estuaries of tidal rivers — but superimposed over it all, like the detail-crowded top sheet of an acetate composite map, lies the other Jersey shore, the elongated summer metropolis paved half with asphalt and half with pizza crusts, culminating — after a brief and incongruous respite at the Barnegat Wildlife Refuge — in the casinos of Atlantic City.

But Sandy Hook, the closest of all the Jersey beachlands to New York City, has stayed out of step, has avoided colonization, and is now "home free" under the protection of Gateway National Recreation Area. The reason is both ironic and simple: Sandy Hook is too important a feature of the outer approaches to New York harbor not to have been part of its defenses. Thus, over a space of 184 years, the federal government acquired and managed most of this fragile, shifting finger of land for use as a fort and as an ordnance proving ground. Even the most ardent pacifist would have to admit that it fared better in the hands of

the military than it might have done with those who fashioned the rest of the Jersey shore.

With its 221-year-old light, visible 19 miles out to sea, Sandy Hook has long stood sentry at the entrance to the harbor. It seems incredible that the waters off the Hook have never been the scene of some desperate naval battle, with New York as the prize, but that is the way history has gone. Sandy Hook missed its one big chance to join the ranks of Lepanto, Trafalgar, and Midway because of the hesitation to fight shown by a French admiral (although some blame his subordinates) during the American Revolution.

This is how this almost-but-not-quite confrontation developed: early in 1777, the British, who held New York City throughout the war, sent their 26th Regiment to seize Sandy Hook and fortify it with a five-gun battery. This accomplished, the Royal Navy was safe to maneuver off the coast. In July of the following year, Admiral Richard "Black Dick" Howe anchored near the Hook with seven ships, totaling 327 guns, in anticipation of the arrival of a French fleet. The French had just joined the war on the American side; the colonists had been relieved to learn that Admiral Comte d'Estaing had sailed from France with the heavily armed men o'war so necessary to the pursual of a successful coast campaign.

On July 11, 1778, d'Estaing arrived off Sandy Hook. The French fleet numbered twelve ships, with a complement of 856 guns. This gave d'Estaing a decided edge over Howe in firepower, but the topography of the ocean bottom kept the issue moot. An undersea sand bar blocked the French from sailing to within range of Howe's vessels. The depth of the water over the bar was a scant 23 feet, and most of d'Estaing's ships had a 25-foot draft. So a standoff developed. When, after a few days, a higher than usual tide enabled the French to cross the bar, Howe stood off the Hook and waited. And waited. For all the French admiral seemed to care, he might be waiting there still, blocking tanker traffic bound for the Arthur Kill. Rather than engaging the smaller, lightly armed formation of British ships,

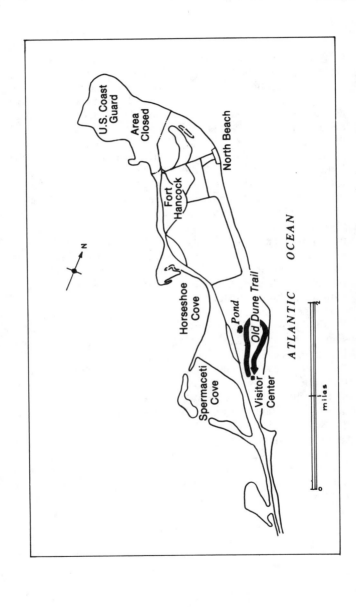

d'Estaing inexplicably turned his fleet southwards and out of sight. This was the beginning of a year-long campaign during which the colonists were repeatedly exasperated by the vacillation of the French naval commander. D'Estaing was, by most accounts, a brave man (he was wounded in a later revolutionary encounter), but he was never known for striking while the iron was hot.

After the Revolution, Sandy Hook was left largely to the lighthouse keeper, a handful of hardy and idiosyncratic settlers (one traveler, in 1879, found a family living in a beached canal boat), and a small annual detachment of tourists. Regular inhabitants also included the men of the lifesaving service, whose vigilance reflected the danger associated with the harbor approaches in the days of sailing ships. The service's 1894 station, near Spermaceti Cove, is today's Gateway Visitor Center. The building contains early lifesaving paraphernalia, as well as interpretive displays touching on all aspects of the peninsula's natural and human history.

Peninsula? Yes, at present. But a look at the physical past of Sandy Hook reveals why settlement there has always been sparse and sporadic. The original Dutch name was "Sand Punt," or sand point, which indicates that the first European settlers found it attached to the mainland. But over the centuries that followed, Sandy Hook has been playing an irregular game of tag with the rest of New Jersey. When General Howe (the admiral's brother) retreated from the battle of Monmouth in 1778, he reached the Hook by bridge. A 1784 chart illustrates this breach in the spit. By 1800, the land bridge had re-formed; by 1830, it was gone. But when a railroad to Horseshoe Cove was built in 1864, the tracks were laid along dry land. (Rail service continued until 1893.) Today, of course, Sandy Hook continues to be a full-fledged peninsula — but the Atlantic's currents and tides, along with the Shrewsbury and Navesink Rivers, are no doubt still capable of treating the "punt" with caprice.

Throughout these years of tenuous connection with the mainland, the shape and size of Sandy Hook have changed. In 1764, what is now the oldest lighthouse on the Atlantic coast was built here. It stood 500 feet from the Hook's northern tip. By 1880, nearly a mile separated the light from the tip, and since then another half mile has been added. The phenomenon responsible for this relentless stretching of the peninsula is called "littoral drift." The process is simple: the ocean's longshore currents sweep sand away from the Hook's exposed flank, and deposit it at the tip. Meanwhile, sand carried southwards by lesser currents in the bay is slowly filling in Spermaceti Cove. A map of Sandy Hook is writ, littorally, in sand.

As we noted earlier, the federal government long ago realized the defensive importance of this delicate piece of land. After a long history of intermittent fortification, work was begun on a permanent installation in 1858. This battery and its attendant structures was commissioned as Fort Hancock in 1895 and remained active until 1974, by which time its Nike missile silos and their contents had become obsolete. But Fort Hancock was famous not for the shots which it fired in anger, but as the site of the Army Ordnance Proving Ground from 1874 to 1919. Thousands of rounds of heavy ammunition were lobbed about here during this period, and it was the discovery of a number of unexploded shells in parts of the old testing area that occasioned the closing of park property on Sandy Hook late in 1979. Visitors can expect to see several signs that read as follows:

WARNING
Military Explosives
Have Been Found in this Area.
If Any Suspicious Objects Are
Found Contact Park Personnel.
DO NOT
Attempt to Move Them.
Many are Extremely Dangerous.

Forewarned is forearmed. In the unlikely event that you happen upon one of these "suspicious objects," remember that they were designed for the Kaiser's fleet, and not your family room.

The grounds and some of the buildings of the fort proper are now open to the public. Call 201-872-0115 for schedules of guided tours, or pick up an entrance booklet and self-guided tour booklet at the Visitor Center. Highlights are Officers' Row; the parade ground; the barracks; and the 20-inch Rodman gun, which is the largest muzzle-loading smoothbore cannon you will ever see.

The naturalist need not travel as far as the military historian to appreciate Sandy Hook. The nearer reaches of the 10-mile peninsula, from the Gateway entrance to the fort, are home to a surprisingly varied plant community, and offer excellent birding opportunities. The natural phenomenon the visitor least expects is perhaps the holly forest. Holly is particularly suited to the sandy soil here, and its tough leaves can survive exposure to the harsh salt air. This is a virgin stand; the oldest trees have been growing for over 150 years. Before you look around for gargantuan hollies, though, remember that this species adds only one inch to its diameter every 10 or 15 years. Thus even the most modest specimens are likely to be older than most visitors to Sandy Hook.

The densest concentration of hollies is along the western shore of the peninsula, near Horseshoe Cove. This area has been set aside as a wildlife preserve, and as such is closed to unguided visitors. There are guided tours of the preserve on Saturdays throughout the year; call ahead for details.

Another plant oddly indigenous to Sandy Hook is the prickly pear cactus. These little succulents, which appreciate the well-drained oceanside soil as they do that of the desert, can be found along many of the area's trails. In autumn, the cacti produce an edible red fruit. Bayberry and beach plum also grow here in profusion, as does another plant — poison ivy. If you walk the trails for diversion during a day otherwise spent on the beach, bring along shoes, socks, and long slacks.

Waterfowl abound at Sandy Hook, especially during spring and fall migration seasons. While the areas adjacent to the salt marshes on the bay side of the peninsula are likely spots to find ducks, geese, and occasionally brant (osprey also nest here), serious birders might seek permission to visit one of the five freshwater ponds that lie within the Gateway boundaries. All of the ponds are well concealed by thicket; at least one was not discovered until aerial photographs were taken. All were formed when hollows were left filled with seawater after irruptions of the ocean. Gradually, upper layers of fresh water supplanted the seawater, with the bird, plant, and small animal life that make up the pond ecosystem following soon after.

PUBLIC TRANSIT: From the Port Authority terminal in New York, take the Academy bus line to the last stop in Highlands, New Jersey. The walk from Highlands is three miles. The Visitor Center (and beginning of trails) is two miles from the entrance.

AUTOMOBILE: Take the Holland Tunnel to the New Jersey Turnpike, and the Turnpike south to the Garden State Parkway. Get off of the parkway at exit 117, and follow Route 36 to Highlands and the park entrance.

THE WALK: Because of fragile dune environments and concern for the well-being of the holly forest/wildlife preserve, Gateway officials request that visitors walk along marked trails, self-guiding brochures for which are available at the Visitor Center. Principal marked trails include the Old Dune Trail, which winds past a dense growth of prickly pear cactus into a holly forest (not the larger preserve forest), skirts the former Nike missile site (now overgrown), and heads toward the ocean beach, and the South Beach Dune Trail (uninterpreted), located on the left side of the road leading to Parking Lot F.

SANDY HOOK

There is a beach parking fee of $2.00 per motorized vehicle ($3.00 on weekends and holidays) in effect from the Saturday of Memorial Day weekend through Labor Day. This fee applies to all beach parking lots designated with a "U.S. Fee Area" sign. Parking at Fort Hancock is free.

6

THE HACKENSACK MEADOWS

Walking — 2 to 5 miles, depending on dryness of terrain. For hundreds of years, this vast wetland has defied exploitation; now it is undergoing great changes.

> *Twenty years ago . . . the Jersey marshes — that great area of low land and water which so long stood as a barrier to modern progress in that direction — stretched their uninviting acres to the west . . . . The meadows are still there, but no longer regarded as a worthless waste.*
>
> *— from "Summer in the Palisades," a promotional pamphlet issued by the Northern Railroad of New Jersey, 1875.*

All major attempts to reclaim the Meadows, beginning with the first attempt in 1816, have come to naught so far. . . . Today the Meadows are waiting for the developments that are bound to come.

> *— From* Field Trips in Interesting and Historic New Jersey, *by Bertram P. Boucher and Hugh C. Brooks, 1962.*

In just 7 short years, we turned marshlands into a vital, beautiful world for business and pleasure. . . . We did it — and we're proud!

> *— Advertisement, Hartz Mountain Industries, 1978.*

THE HACKENSACK MEADOWS (sometimes called the New Jersey Meadows, or the Secaucus Meadows, or simply the Meadows) are home to 18 species of ladybug, the largest concentration of muskrat in the metropolitan area, and the football

Giants. And they aren't really "meadows" at all — they are a combination of marshland and tidal estuary, drained by the lower reaches of the Hackensack and Passaic Rivers. These meadows and marshes weren't always wetlands — hundreds of years ago, a cedar forest stood here. The land was inundated by rising water levels in Newark Bay, and the present ecology, in a much healthier form, became predominant. Today, the lower Hackensack and its meandering tributaries are distinctly tidal, as is evident to any Meadows canoeist who spends more than a few hours on the water.

Nothing contributes so much to the misnomer "Meadows" as the area's major plant species, *phragmites communis*. To anyone standing on the heights of Jersey City, or along the ridges to the west, the Hackensack Valley appears as a virtually unbroken sea of this tall, tenacious grass. Although phragmites in such abundance are proof of man's incursions upon such an expansive natural wetland and are poor providers of food for wildlife, the plant's ubiquitousness and phenomenal growing habits make it worth some interest.

Phragmites communis (the name comes from the Greek words for "fence" and "in colonies") is capable of reproducing from seed, although that is rarely the means by which it spreads. Instead, it relies upon a tough, rhizomatous root system, capable of extending 50 feet within a single season. The bulbous portions of these rhizomes, incidentally, can be boiled and eaten like potatoes, but this is not recommended in an area that has been subjected to as much industrial and solid waste pollution as the Jersey Meadows. I haven't tried them myself, but the young green shoots are also reportedly edible, either raw or cooked like asparagus.

The phragmites' method of propagation gives the plant two distinct characteristics: first, it spreads remarkably fast, quickly excluding other, more desirable marsh plants; and second, the underground concealment of its vigorous portions enables it easily to establish itself after fire. A fire ecology actually favors phragmites; the shoots often emerge in concentrations even

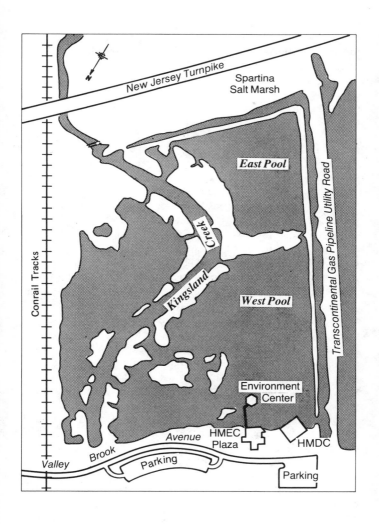

thicker than those of the preceding generation. In some places, controlled burning of phragmites has been undertaken as a means of preventing greater fire hazards in the future. Such measures are unlikely to destroy the plant's culture in the area, though, unless repeated often enough during a single season to deny the root systems the nutrients which would have been derived from photosynthesis. Once phragmites take over, then, they are likely to be around for good.

How do they get their first foothold? Often, phragmites appear in salt marshes that have been denied access to salt water by damming or filling operations, or when the more delicate plants of a salt marsh ecology are decimated by pollutants. Both of these conditions have been met in the Meadows.

Phragmites have their positive side, in addition to their familiar decorative use in dried plant arrangements. The English sometimes use them for thatching roofs. In Russia, they are grown as a cellulose crop for paper production. The stiff reeds make quills for calligraphy. And their tall, dense thickets help give the Meadows their aura of mystery and impenetrability.

But this is an aura, and nothing more. Men have penetrated the Meadows for centuries to fish, crab, hunt waterfowl, build railroads, and, unfortunately, to dump garbage. Perhaps no other human activity — not even the notorious, now-vanished Secaucus pig farms — has given the Meadows such an unsavory reputation. For decades, the prevailing notion in northern New Jersey could be summed up like this: "It's too soft to build on, nobody lives there, and it's right nearby. We've got all this garbage. . . ."

And so the trucks came, disgorged themselves of trash, and left, in a cycle that contaminated more and more of the Meadows. Finally, civic repulsion with the eggshell-and-coffee-grounds (and worse) school of wetlands use, combined with the sudden realization that here was a real estate gold mine, led to the first official attempt at the zoning and planned development of the Meadows. The result was the state-chartered Hackensack Meadowlands Development Commission (HMDC), which has been guiding the area's growth since 1968.

The colonization of the Meadows, alternately predicted and dismissed as impossible for centuries, began in earnest during the mid-1970s. New fill and construction techniques made building possible where it was previously out of the question, and the Meadows' 5- to 200-foot-deep stratum of unconsolidated silt and muck is no longer an insurmountable engineering problem. The prospect of a former wetland bustling with industry, sports, and home construction, of course, cannot be faced with unmitigated glee. But consider: had not the planners come to the Meadows, the dumpers and random developers would have won the place by default. Whatever one's reservations about the scale of some HMDC projects — certain of which seem grandiose, to say the least — there is no contesting the fact that more than a decade of supervised development has worked some welcome reversals in the Meadows. Water quality in the Hackensack has steadily improved, as has the overall marsh ecology. Shellfish have been returning, and the river now supports 36 species of fish. Marsh hawks breed here once again. Two hundred and seventy other avian species have been spotted over the estuary.

This clean-up effort was not without its incentives. If the state, working through the commission with private developers, wanted to attract recreationists, condominium buyers, and big-name corporations into the Meadows (and onto the tax rolls), something had to be done about the area's garbage-dump-*cum*-sewer image.

Using the powers given it by the state, the HMDC has restricted the flow of pollutants into Meadows waterways. The Hackensack had long been the recipient not only of industrial wastes and spills, but of raw or poorly treated sewage and the toxic chemicals leached from the surrounding acres of garbage. New regulations forbid discharge of certain substances into the river and specify diking around landfills. Sewage treatment plants have been built and expanded around the Hackensack basin. A vigorous monitoring system has been set up, so that lapses and improvements in water quality may be recognized. Finally, a timetable has been established for elimination of the open dumping of solid wastes into the Meadows.

Although there have been repeated extensions (as of this writing, dumping continues practically within sight of the DeKorte Park headquarters), it seems as if the procession of garbage trucks will finally stop in 1988. The Commission's zoning requirements are designed to make the Meadows into as attractive a development setting as possible, while maintaining good environmental standards and setting aside a reasonable measure of open land. Toward this latter end, they have stipulated that 50 percent of the property to be occupied by any new project be left open. Individual developers have responded by coming up with a variety of park- and preservation-oriented designs, but the best hope for maintaining a significant, uninterrupted stretch of the old Meadows lies with the Commission's plans for Richard DeKorte State Park, sections of which are already open.

DeKorte is a multiple-use park. In its final form it should include both a wildlife management area and developed sections with hiking, nature-observation, and recreational facilities. A nature-study center, hiking trails, and raised boardwalks are already in place; future development calls for the reclaiming and landscaping of present-day landfill areas. There are numerous places from which to observe the protected marshland, ranging from the glassed-in east wing of the nature center to soggy pathways for which wading boots may be borrowed without charge. Binoculars may also be borrowed at the nature center.

Anyone new to the Meadows should be advised that not everything to be seen there, even on some sections of the park property, is "pretty" in the sense that we come to expect of nature on our weekend rambles. Parts of it look like a swamp wilderness; parts look like a dump. It is nonetheless a fascinating place, especially at this stage in its history. Perhaps it is sad to see what had until recently been a reedy, creek-threaded no-man's-land finally charted and planned into submission. But

the future of the Meadows was rapidly narrowing into two options: wild, filthy, and polluted; or tame and reasonably clean. What about wild and clean? It couldn't happen. Look east, past the railroad bridges. There are counting-houses there a thousand feet tall.

PUBLIC TRANSIT: New Jersey Transit buses Nos. 191 and 192 leave New York's Port Authority Terminal for Lyndhurst weekdays between 7 and 8:30 AM and return to New York from Lyndhurst between 4 and 5:15 PM. There is no service on weekends. From New York, take the bus to the Lyndhurst Corporate Center and get off at the corner of Chubb and Valley Brook avenues. To reach the DeKorte Park Nature Center, walk to the end of Valley Brook Avenue.

AUTOMOBILE: From New York, take the Lincoln Tunnel to Route 3 west and exit onto Route 17 south. At the first traffic light (look for the Quality Inn), take the Polito Avenue exit and continue to Valley Brook Avenue. Turn left and drive to the end of Valley Brook Avenue.

THE WALK: Trails and boardwalks at DeKorte Park are still under development as of this writing. One popular walk, around the marshes surrounding Kingsland Creek, takes about an hour and begins at the nature center. Turn left as you leave the center (maps are available at the main desk) and then left again onto the right-of-way of the buried Transco gas pipeline. The west and east pools of the Kingsland Creek marshes will be on your left. After ¼ mile you'll see the New Jersey Turnpike ahead; turn left here and follow the gravel road, crossing Kingsland Creek and reaching the Conrail tracks. If you turn right here, you can walk along the tracks (be careful!) to the Hackensack River. Turning left, you will reach Valley Brook Avenue, which is the access road to the park headquarters and nature center. Turn left onto Valley Brook Avenue to return to your starting point.

A more ambitious walk will be possible upon completion of the "Meadows Path," which will stretch from Little Ferry, in Bergen County, to Kearny, in Hudson County. Some sections of this 11-mile route are already in place; check at the DeKorte nature center concerning accessibility.

7

MORRISTOWN NATIONAL HISTORICAL PARK

A walk into American Revolutionary history, with visits to the eighteenth-century mansion where George Washington once made his headquarters and to the campgrounds of the Continental Army during the devastating winter of 1779-80.

New JERSEY HAS JUSTLY BEEN CALLED the cockpit of the American Revolution. True, the first shots of the insurrection were fired at Lexington and Concord, and the first major battle was fought at Bunker Hill (Breed's Hill, to be exact), in Charlestown, Massachusetts. But once the war was under way, the principal theater of operations was the woods and farmlands of the colony that lay between British-occupied New York and the seat of the Continental Congress in Philadelphia. The game of fox and hounds that began with Washington's retreat from New York in 1776 (see Chapters 14 and 15) was played largely on New Jersey soil for the next four years.

Skirmishes such as Trenton, Princeton, and Springfield notwithstanding, though, Jersey in the late 1770s wasn't a scene of constant fighting. Warfare in the eighteenth century was largely a matter of waiting out the weather, and winter encampments with all their attendant tedium and hardship were a necessary part of military strategy. The most familiar tales of winter bivouac and the toll it took on the Continental army came out of Valley Forge, where Washington's forces were quartered in the winter of 1777-78. But before and after Valley Forge — during the winter of 1776-77, and again in 1779-80 — the rebel forces

made winter camp at Morristown, New Jersey. The places where they drilled and froze and waited are preserved for us today, in the two major sections of Morristown National Historical Park.

General Washington first brought his army to Morristown in January 1777, just after his dramatic Christmas crossing of the Delaware at Trenton and January 3 rout of the British at Princeton. The shire town of Morris County, at that time a village of about fifty houses, appeared to the commander-in-chief to be an ideal place to await the replenishment of his forces (through new enlistments) while holding a defensible and strategically sound position — protected from the main British army at New York and north coastal New Jersey by the natural barriers of the Great Swamp and the Watchung Mountains. But the hoped-for enlistments failed to materialize, at least not in numbers sufficient to replace those soldiers being mustered out at the end of their one-year terms of service, and Washington resigned himself to spending the winter with his men in and around the little Jersey town. It was, after all, a productive agricultural area, and provisions were not hard to come by. There were also iron mines and forges nearby, all of them in friendly hands. The commander billeted his men in local households and took up his own headquarters at the Arnold Tavern, on the village green, on January 6.

Washington's army remained in Morristown and environs until the end of May, by which time the rebels' strength in the area had increased to about 10,000 men, though no more than three quarters of them were ready for any sort of immediate action. But there was no immediate action in the offing. The army moved south toward New Brunswick, where the British commander, Lord Howe, had marched, ostensibly in order to goad Washington's smaller force into battle. When this stratagem failed (Washington knew stacked odds when he saw them), Howe began moving his troops back toward Staten Island, completing what amounted to a more or less voluntary evacua-

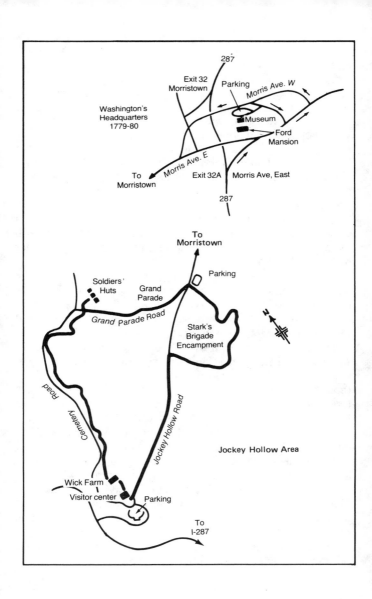

tion of New Jersey by the end of June. Even given the cautious nature of Revolutionary War-era campaigning, this diffidence on the part of Howe is hard to fathom. It wasn't until mid-August, after the Continental Army had spent most of the summer in north central New Jersey stymied by the absence of a visible opponent, that Howe's next objective became apparent. He had brought his men by ship through Chesapeake Bay to the southern threshhold of Philadelphia. Howe marched north, Washington south, and the two armies met at Brandywine Creek on September 11. The result was a debacle for the colonists. Washington's forces were routed, Philadelphia was occupied by the British (the Continental Congress escaped to the west), and — after yet another loss for the colonists at Germantown in October — the stage was set for the Continental army's winter bivouac at Valley Forge.

Morristown does not again figure in the narrative of the Revolution until two winters after the Valley Forge encampment of 1777-78. The intervening years saw no major action, and the winter of 1778-79 found the Continental army scattered in a rough crescent across north Jersey, southern New York, and western Connecticut. But as 1779 drew to a close, the idea of safe winter billeting in a single spot again appeared attractive to the commander, and Morristown was the place. This time, though, there would be 10,000 men camped behind the protective flank of the Watchungs, and they would live not in the homes of local farmers but in a log-hut city of their own making.

The troops began arriving in the early part of December 1779, and on the face of it they had a far more comfortable winter ahead of them than the one they had spent at Valley Forge. There was more food at hand, as well as an improved — if by no means wholly adequate — system for supplying such things as clothing and blankets. But there was one variable they hadn't planned on, and it struck with a vengeance even before the main body of Continental soldiers had arrived and settled in. The winter of 1779-80 was to be the worst of the eighteenth century, with more than two dozen separate storms leaving nine feet of snow in the Morristown area. Roads were not only rendered impassable but were entirely obscured, as drifts obliterated even the fences that bordered them. There was food in the area, but as far as wagons or even sleds were concerned it may as well have been in California. At times, it must have seemed as if nature itself had gone over to the Loyalists' side.

In spite of the snow and cold — one imagines men spending more time shoveling than building — the army managed to clear 600 acres in a place called Jockey Hollow, some four miles from the village of Morristown. There they built between 1,000 and 1,200 log huts, in neat rows descending toward a common parade ground. Some half-dozen of these huts have been accurately reconstructed at Jockey Hollow, and what you see there is what the men saw, twelve to a hut, throughout that long winter: wooden bunks heaped with straw for bedding, a single door and window, and a stone hearth to supply all they would have of heat and light. Given the circumstances, it is astounding that only 86 men died from illness, hunger, and cold, and that there were no serious flirtations with mutiny until springtime was near.

As is true in any age, the commander-in-chief did not live in quite the same fashion as the enlisted men. Washington made his Morristown headquarters at the Ford Mansion, by far the most imposing of the village's houses. It belonged to Theodosia Ford, the widow of Jacob Ford, an owner of iron mines in the district. By Jockey Hollow standards, the accommodations at the Ford Mansion were luxurious, but the squire of Mount Vernon and commander of the Continental army no doubt occasionally felt cramped, since the mansion housed not only him and (after December 31) Mrs. Washington, but also Mrs. Ford and her four children, the Ford and Washington family servants, and a military headquarters staff of between ten and twenty men. On the grounds nearby were log buildings, hastily thrown up to house the 250 members of Washington's Life Guard. All in all, the Ford Mansion amounted to an elegant Georgian barracks, but a barracks nonetheless.

Today's visitors to the mansion will no doubt look at the

lovely Queen Anne highboys, great kitchen hearth, and dining table set with porcelain and Madeira and conclude that this wouldn't be a bad place to hole up for a season. But even with fireplaces blazing, indoor temperatures during the terrible winter of 1779-80 probably hovered around 40°F. And the privy was out in the yard.

Nor was the winter season at the Morristown headquarters simply a round of candlelit balls and genteel afternoon strategy sessions over glasses of Madeira. Washington and his officers had to work hard to cope with supply logistics, community relations (10,000 billeted soldiers won't always get along splendidly with the local yeomen), military intelligence, and the planning of minor forays — as well as the coming year's strategy. The campaign of 1780 would mark the sixth summer of the war, and the one in which French assistance to the rebels would finally, though slowly, begin to materialize. Washington received a pair of French emissaries in April, and on May 10 the Marquis de Lafayette arrived at Morristown to announce that a French expeditionary force was on its way.

Men and supplies were finally moved away from Morristown in late June of 1780. At about the same time, a detachment of Continentals held off the British near Springfield, New Jersey, and the British army — now under the generalship of Sir Henry Clinton — left the colony for good in favor of their Staten Island stronghold. The bulk of the Continental army then moved toward the Hudson highlands, and the war moved toward its denouement, sixteen months and another tedious winter later, at Yorktown. Only a few small detachments of the Colonial forces were to camp in the Morristown huts during that winter of 1780-81, and fewer still (fittingly, the New Jersey Brigade) the following year. The Ford Mansion went back to being the seat of a provincial New Jersey family, and trees grew again in Jockey Hollow as the log town the troops had built fell into ruin.

Fortunately, time was kind to both places. The mansion was acquired in 1873 by a private group, which evolved into the

Washington Association and eventually turned the property over to the federal government. By the 1920s, sentiment was also running strong for the preservation of the still-open land at Jockey Hollow and the nearby promontory on which the Continentals' observation post of "Fort Nonsense" had stood. In 1932, the parcels were combined to form the first National Historical Park.

PUBLIC TRANSIT: The Ford Mansion, museum, and park headquarters may be reached via New Jersey Transit buses leaving from New York's Port Authority Building. Get off the bus at the parking lot near the museum. Returning, board buses across Morris Avenue from the Ford Mansion, or at Morristown Green. New Jersey Transit trains from Hoboken stop at Morristown station, one block west of the mansion/museum complex. There is no public transportation to Jockey Hollow.

AUTOMOBILE: Take Interstate 80 west to Interstate 287; head south to Morristown and take exit 32, following signs for park headquarters. After visiting the museum and Ford Mansion, continue to Jockey Hollow (where the trail system begins) by getting back on Interstate 287 southbound to the Route 202 exit, where you will see signs directing you to the park.

Be sure to allow a couple of hours for your visit to the museum and Ford Mansion. The museum houses an impressive collection of Revolutionary-era weapons, furnishings, and personal possessions and offers informative film presentations. It's also the starting point for guided tours of the Ford Mansion, which has been restored to its appearance at the time of Washington's occupancy and furnished accordingly, though in most cases not with original Ford family artifacts.

Visiting Jockey Hollow is more of an outdoor experience.

Near the parking area is a small interpretive center, from which a short walk takes you to the Wick House, a sturdy New England-style eighteenth-century farmhouse used as a head-quarters by General Arthur St. Clair during the 1779-80 encampment. Authentic down to its gardens, the house speaks volumes about the life led by a relatively prosperous farm family at the time of the Revolution.

THE WALK: From the Wick House, a walk of about 1½ miles along Cemetery Road or the adjacent path takes you to Grand Parade Field and the reconstructed soldiers' huts. You may return to the Wick House and Visitor Center the same way, or fork right onto Grand Parade Road, which leads to Jockey Hollow Road. Turn right onto Jockey Hollow Road to return to the Visitor Center, or left to reach a right-hand turn onto the trail that loops through the 1779-80 encampment site of General John Stark's brigade, before rejoining Jockey Hollow Road (left at this point for Visitor Center).

The above-mentioned routes comprise only a small portion of the 26 miles of hiking trails at Jockey Hollow and the adjoining Lewis Morris County Park and Scherman-Hoffman Audubon Sanctuary. Of particular interest is Patriots' Path, a part-completed trail which planners hope will eventually link Jockey Hollow and points west in Mendham Township with East Hanover and the Essex County Center for Environmental Studies in Roseland (see Chapter 3). A completed section of the trail extends from the New Jersey Brigade encampment site at the southern extreme of the National Park, through Jockey Hollow and past the soldiers' huts to Sunrise Lake on Route 24. Maps of all the area's trails are available at the Jockey Hollow Visitor Center; for specific information on Patriots' Path, contact the Friends of Patriots' Path, 300 Mendham Road, Morristown, NJ 07960 (201-539-7540).

MORRISTOWN

Morristown National Historical Park, Morristown, New Jersey, is open daily except Thanksgiving, Christmas Day, and New Year's Day from 9 AM to 5 PM. Park roads close at sundown. For further information, call 201-539-2085.

8

SANDS POINT

Walking — 7 to 8 miles, including walk from bus stop; 3 to 4 miles of trails within preserve exclusive of walk from bus. Historic houses, exhibits of Americana, nature center, and trails (three are self-guiding) through forest, fields, and along 100-foot cliffs.

LONG ISLAND WAS bequeathed to us by the Wisconsin Ice Sheet, between 30,000 and 50,000 years ago. There was a landmass here before that — the glacier had to have something to work with — but we would hardly have recognized it as it was then. There certainly would have been no Montauk, no Fire Island, no Lake Ronkonkoma, and no Sands Point.

Sands Point is a peninsula protruding into Long Island Sound between Manhasset Bay and Hempstead Harbor. It lies just to the north of the Harbor Hill moraine, which defines the southern limit of the last glacial advance in this area. Although the point is not part of the moraine itself, its topographical appearance was largely defined by the ice sheet during the time of its withdrawal from Long Island. Thirty thousand years is but an instant in the course of natural history, and we can read the story of the glacier's departure along the trails in the Sands Point Preserve.

Perhaps we should backtrack a few eons first, though. Long before the coming of the glaciers, what is now the central trough of Long Island Sound had been carved out by an ancient river. Other streams emptied into this river, cutting their own paths as they did so. That is why the shore of the modern sound is so

irregular, and why there is a Manhasset Bay and a Hempstead Harbor to set off Sands Point. The level of the sea was not sufficiently high to drown this river system, because so much of the world's water had been drawn upon in the formation of an early, pre-Wisconsin glacier. This glacier moved south, but it never reached the sound. Instead, it began to recede and melt over what is now southern Connecticut. The detritus released by its southward-flowing meltwaters were deposited over what is now the floor of the sound.

So things remained until the Wisconsin Ice Sheet arrived. This glacier pushed farther, gouging the sound bed and piling its gravel, along with material collected between Labrador and New England, into the heap now known as the Ronkonkoma moraine. Thus the more southerly of Long Island's two rock ribs was created, and, along with it, Montauk Point. The glacier then retreated, but not for long. A second advance terminated in the formation of the Harbor Hill moraine, which parallels, and toward the west merges with, the earlier Ronkonkoma formation.

This final cessation of glacial movement, along with the atmospheric warming which followed, marked the beginning of our own era. The lands to the south of the dual moraine on Long Island became what geologists call an "outwash plain" — a vast repository of debris sifted, sorted, and carried seawards by streams issuing from the melting glacier. North of the moraines the meltwater from the ebbing ice sheet filled the sound, leaving similar deposits of outwash and randomly collected, unsorted material called "glacial till" throughout the north shore. Large boulders were also left. These are called "erratics"; one is visible along the purple-blazed, self-guiding trail No. 4 at Sands Point. Now it was the sea's turn to play land builder, and it has been doing so for centuries by means of its most dependable and relentless process — erosion. If you take the shoreline trail at Sands Point Park (marked No. 5 on maps, and blazed in blue), you will walk along the base of 100-foot cliffs whose eroded faces reveal the layers of outwash and till accumulated by the

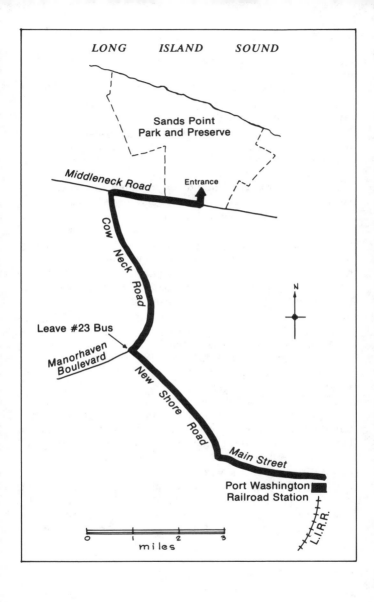

cutting edge of the glacier, and left here in the days of its dissolution.

Human history, of course, eventually intervened, though never on so grandiose a scale as during the estate-building period at the beginning of our own century. Sands Point's 230 acres, like the lands occupied by the Bayard Cutting and Planting Fields Arboretums, came into public ownership after years spent as the summer estate of a wealthy family. Two families, to be exact — this accounts for the double complement of mansions on the grounds. The property belonged to railroad heir Howard Gould at the turn of the century; it was he who built the Tudor-inspired Hempstead House and "Castlegould," the enormous turreted stable which now serves as a visitor center and home of the Nassau County Museum's Americana Storage Study Collections. But Gould moved to Europe without ever having lived in the main house, and in 1917 the Daniel Guggenheim family purchased the estate. In 1923 Harry Guggenheim, Daniel's son, built the Norman mansion "Falaise" (from the French word for cliff) on his share of the family property. Both Hempstead House (used by the government as regional naval defense headquarters during World War II, and as a naval training devices center from 1946 to 1967) and Falaise are open to visitors via escorted tours; reservations are suggested for the Falaise tour. For schedules, call the park at 516-883-1612.

The Nassau County Department of Recreation and Parks manages Sands Point not only as a focus of historical interest, but for the preservation and public enjoyment of its natural features. There are five marked trails (three are self-guiding), all of which can be leisurely walked within a half-day's time. In addition to the geological phenomena mentioned above, there is a wide range of plant and bird life within the preserve. Over 300 botanical species thrive here, several of which are on the New York state protected plant list and are found in only two or three other locations on Long Island. The largest American elm and the second largest black oak on Long Island are found along the No. 2 trail (red blazes). Fall wildflowers are abundant; these

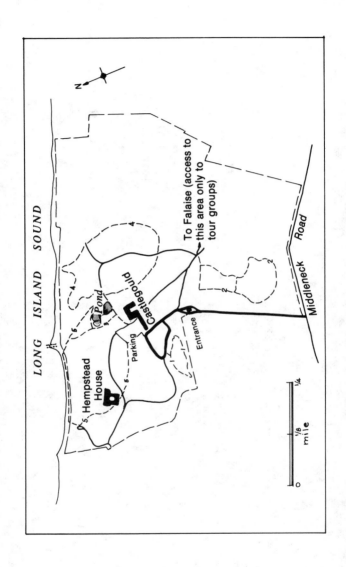

include white wood aster, white snakewood, soapwort, yarrow, "butter·and eggs," goldenrod, vine honeysuckle, and Asiatic dayflower. Among Sands Point bird species are the bank swallow, which nests in holes in the eroding cliffs; belted kingfisher, sometimes observed diving at the small pond near the beginning of trail No. 4; and cormorants, both great (winter) and double crested (summer). Two species that benefit from the park policy of allowing lawns to grow full before cutting are the meadowlark and bobolink, both of which have been decreasing elsewhere within their traditional range because of steady habitat loss.

Sands Point Preserve, 95 Middleneck Road, Port Washington, New York, is open mid-April through mid-November. Hours are 10 AM to 4:30 PM Mondays, Tuesdays, Wednesdays, Saturdays, and Sundays. The park is closed on Thursdays and Fridays. Vehicle admission is $1.00; additional fees are charged for special tours.

PUBLIC TRANSIT: Take the Long Island Railroad to the Port Washington station, where you can connect with the No. 23 bus north on Main Street to New Shore Road. Get off at the corner of New Shore Road and Manorhaven Boulevard, and turn right onto Cow Neck Road where it intersects with New Shore Road. Walk north on Cow Neck Road to Middleneck Road and turn right. Entrance to park is fourth left. (Approximately 2 miles.)

AUTOMOBILE: Take the Long Island Expressway to exit 36. Drive north on Searingtown Road, which changes its name to Port Washington Road and then to Middleneck Road. Entrance to park is on your right, just north of Port Washington village.

THE WALK: Pick up trail maps at the visitor center in Castlegould. Trails 4 and 5 are especially recommended; trails 1 and 3 are short loops ideal for small children.

9

PLANTING FIELDS ARBORETUM

Walking — 6 to 7 miles, including walk from Oyster Bay train station; 2 to 3 miles without. Arboretum and greenhouses; collection is particularly strong in maples, camellias, and flowering shrubs, although many varied species are represented.

OF ALL THE TREE species which grow at Planting Fields Arboretum, in Oyster Bay on the north shore of Long Island, the most fascinating may be one which is not enumerated in the self-guiding tour brochures, not immediately recognized for its stately profiles or October pyrotechnics, and not really present at all, save in the shape of a few doomed saplings. It was once a predominant feature of the northeastern landscape; now, it exists here and in other forest pockets as a ghost tree, in the shadows between extinction and revival.

Don't give up; you know the tree. Longfellow's smithy stood under its spreading branches. Your grandmother stuffed turkeys with the kernels of its fruit. And you cannot walk the sidewalks of New York in winter without being proffered the crop of its Italian cousin. The American chestnut, long dead of blight, grows at Planting Fields.

But then again it doesn't. The tree is not extinct, exactly, but neither is the blight which erased it from its old range. The two co-exist in a bizarre symbiosis, which authorities at the arboretum hope will finally be broken. If it is, perhaps mature chestnuts will stand here once again.

Here is what happens: the American chestnut is vulnerable to a fungus, commonly called the chestnut blight, which attacks

the furrows in its bark as they form. Once the fungus takes hold, it girdles and kills the young trees. Since chestnut saplings in their early stages of development are smooth barked, there is a brief time of reprieve; some may even reach the thickness of a man's wrist before succumbing to the blight.

The mature chestnuts of North America disappeared during the first decades of this century. Chestnut saplings, however, can start by suckering from old root systems — thus the species survives although the individuals do not. There are always some living saplings; otherwise the fungus would disappear. Conversely, there is always the fungus; otherwise the mortal cycle would end.

There are two chances for the chestnut's reappearance. The first is that through genetic selection, a blight-resistant variety of the species might appear and reproduce. The second involves human intervention: it is known that there are two strains of the fungus, one weak and the other virulent. Trees stricken with the weaker strain seem to be immune to attacks from the more lethal form. Thus innoculation — deliberate infection of young trees with the mild strain — might be used in an attack on the blight. Natural selection may take many years, and developing and administering a "shot" for the trees may prove extremely costly (it hasn't been tried yet at Planting Fields). Meanwhile, here and in other secluded locations throughout the chestnut's ancient range, the saplings sprout and die.

So it goes with the chestnut. But one visits Planting Fields Arboretum to see the trees that are thriving today. The arboretum's 409 acres contain innumerable specimens, as well as greenhouses and gardens of herbs, flowers, and shrubbery. As with the Bayard Cutting Arboretum (see Chapter 11), the property's focal point is a great mansion reminiscent of Long Island's days as a rich man's retreat, and its intensive ornamental cultivation represents the lifelong enthusiasm of an individual whose means were commensurate with his ends.

The land which Planting Fields occupies has long been noted for its fertility — the arboretum's name, in fact, is a translation

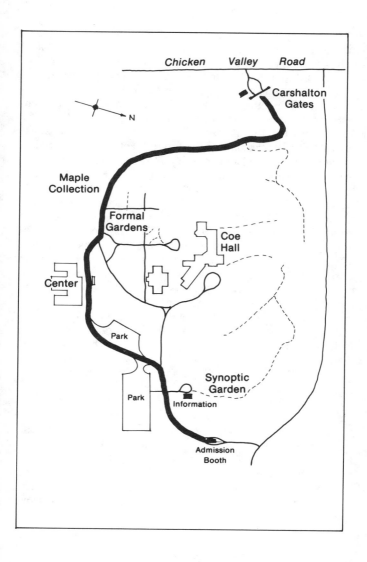

of the name given the area by the Indians, who grew vegetables and tobacco here. The fields' fertile soil is a rich, sandy glacial deposit called Haven loam.

Farming continued on and around Planting Fields throughout the eighteenth and nineteenth centuries. Asparagus and peaches were among the more popular local market crops, and they were also among the last; the north shore of Long Island had, by 1900, attracted the attention of estate-building millionaires. James Byrne began buying the future Planting Fields grounds for an average of $100 per acre in 1904; within two years, a mansion and formal gardens had been completed. But Byrne's tenure was short. The property was purchased by William Robertson Coe, a British-born insurance executive and investor, in 1913. Coe added more land to the estate, and built the present mansion between 1919 and 1921. (Byrne's 1906 structure, which occupied the present site of Coe Hall, had burned in 1918.) Coe began building the greenhouses in 1914. After the camellia collection arrived in 1917, it was discovered that the plants were not hardy enough to survive the winter, and the camellia greenhouse was constructed.

W.R. Coe does not seem to fit the popular image of the north shore plutocrat of the 1920s. Unlike Fitzgerald's heroes, his interests ran to camellias, azaleas, and rhododendrons rather than the gaudier jazz age pleasures. Having revived the old name of "Planting Fields," he applied himself to making the estate a horticultural showplace as well as a productive farm. Until 1935 the property had a working dairy, and pigs and chickens were kept until the 1950s. During the Depression, the Coes donated food and milk to local shelters, and wood and vegetables were sold until Mr. Coe's death in 1955. When Mr. Coe was away (at first he only spent weekends at Planting Fields, but in later life he lived here during spring and fall), he had produce and flowers sent to him from his Long Island estate.

Most of the landscaping at Planting Fields was designed and executed by A. Robeson Sargent, working with Guy Lowell. After Sargent's death in 1918, James Dawson of Olmstead

Brothers took over. The Rose Arbor dates back to Byrne's ownership of the property, but Sargent was responsible for the allees, the vistas near Coe Hall, azalea walks, and — in conjunction with Walker and Gillette, the designers of Coe Hall — the greenhouses. The rhododendron park was not designed until the 1950s.

When it came to planting trees, Coe chose not only promising saplings but went to great ends to acquire and move large, mature specimens as well. The copper beech which stands on the mansion's north lawn was already 60 feet high when it and an identical companion (now dead and removed) were moved from Massachusetts by barge and a team of 72 horses. Two principles apply here. First, beech trees take a long time to grow. Second, patience is a virtue, unless one can afford impatience.

In 1949, Coe arranged for the state to take possession of his property upon his death. Prior to the state's assumption of ownership in 1955, public access to the estate was allowed only once a year, during the peak of the rhododendron season. Even after Coe's death, Mrs. Coe retained life tenancy at Planting Fields. The "Manor House" was built for her in the late 1950s, as she could no longer manage the stairs at Coe Hall.

Today, the Arboretum is aided in its horticultural and public-education roles by the state, by a community organization called the Friends of Planting Fields, and by the Planting Fields Foundation, which was endowed by Mr. Coe. The foundation has been instrumental in maintaining and refurbishing Coe Hall, restoring the camellia greenhouse, and, most recently, commencing the restoration of the main greenhouses, all with the assistance of the state and the Friends of Planting Fields.

One imaginative step taken during the past 30 years has been the planting of the "Synoptic Garden," an assemblage of over 400 species and cultivars of flowering shrubs. This garden, so named because it offers a synopsis of the ornamentals suited for Long Island and the metropolitan area, is arranged in the alphabetical order of the individual specimens. Have you heard of a shrub called Abelia? Zenobia? Here they are, with everything from B to Y tucked artfully between them over five acres of grounds. The azalea walk is a prime springtime attraction, featuring the largest collection of azaleas and rhododendrons in the East. Earlier in the year (January through March), visit the camellia greenhouse, which houses the largest and oldest indoor camellia collection in the United States. There are also a dwarf conifer garden, wildflower meadow, two rhododendron parks, a rose arbor, day-lily collection, and groupings of both English and American hollies. A portion of the grounds has been planted with species providing food and cover for birds, and set aside as a sanctuary. The main greenhouse features non-native varieties, including coffee, pineapple, banana (actually an enormous herb), pomegranates, pygmy date palms, and citrus fruits. The main greenhouse also houses large collections of bromeliads, orchids, begonias, ferns, cacti, and succulents. Caged near the entrance (and evidently feeling quite at home surrounded by the tropical flora) are two bright macaws.

In the renovated Haybarn, near the Arboretum Center and adjacent to the greenhouse complex, is a herbarium containing over 8,500 preserved specimens, as well as a sizeable horticultural library. The herbarium is open by appointment; the library is open Wednesday and Saturday during regular arboretum hours. The Haybarn is also the site of a regular concert series. Coe Hall itself is open to the public May through September on Tuesdays, Wednesdays, and Thursdays from 1 PM to 4 PM, and for special occasions.

Planting Fields is open daily from 9 AM until 5 PM. Admission is $1.50 per person; during the winter season (November through mid-April), it is charged on Saturdays, Sundays, and holidays only. Children under 12 are admitted free. For further information, call 516-922-9200.

PUBLIC TRANSIT: Take the Long Island Railroad to the Oyster Bay station. Walk down Audrey Avenue (street opposite station), bearing left at the fork where several can-

nons are mounted in a grassy triangle, and head up Spring Street to West Main Street. Turn right onto West Main Street, continue past the pond, and turn left onto Lake Avenue. At the T intersection where Lake Avenue meets Glen Cove Road, turn right, and continue on Glen Cove Road until you see the arboretum entrance sign on your left. (Total distance 1.9 miles.)

AUTOMOBILE: Take the Long Island Expressway to exit 41N (or the Northern State Parkway to exit 35N), and follow Route 106 north to Rte. 25A. Turn left on 25A, and make the first right onto Mill River Road. Go north 2 miles, and follow the signs to the arboretum.

THE WALK: It is possible, within a day's time, to make a thorough circuit of the grounds of Planting Fields Arboretum. Individuals interested in a more detailed study of specific horticultural subjects, of course, can easily pass a day or even longer in one of the gardens or greenhouses without losing sight of their starting point. It is suggested that visitors head first for the Arboretum Center, just beyond the second parking lot, to obtain a map showing the location of the principal gardens and walkways; the map in this book provides a general idea of the layout of the grounds. The arboretum staff has prepared a self-guided walking tour (guide booklet available at the center), which takes in 27 of Planting Fields' most outstanding individual trees. Each tree has a yellow marker; the plants along the way are also identified. Another pleasant walk begins at the center, continues along the estate's original drive for ¾ mile, past the formal gardens (right) and the maple collection (left), and ends at the intricate, hand-wrought ironwork of the Carshalton Gates. The gates, which extend for 113 feet, were crafted for Carshalton Park, England in 1712. After the First World War, they were put up for sale,

*and W.R. Coe bought them for Planting Fields. No doubt
he was pleased to have this souvenir of his native England
to welcome him home after a day in the city.*

Quite lovely, these Carshalton Gates, as is all of the arboretum.
Now, if only there were some spreading chestnut trees. . . .

10

RINGWOOD STATE PARK

Walking — 3 to 10 miles. From Borough Hall in Ringwood to Ringwood Manor House and vicinity, with trails to Shepherd Pond, Skylands Manor, and Bear Swamp Lake. A look at the way of life of the masters of one of America's early iron mines, and a walk through the wooded uplands of the New Jersey-New York border.

In FRONT OF RINGWOOD Manor House lie twenty-six links of an enormous iron chain. The chain encircles nothing; there is nothing that it keeps in or keeps out. But this is not a fanciful and titanic lawn ornament. These three-hundred-pound iron loops literally and figuratively represent the vital connection between the Ramapo Valley iron mines and the desperate American Revolutionary War Effort.

From the early eighteenth century down nearly to our own time, Ringwood meant iron. Long before the Mesabi Range of the upper midwest was discovered, the mines of New Jersey and southern New York supplied high-grade ore to the foundries of colonial America and the early republic. And here, the demands of the new industrial order met with the methods of the feudal past to build a manor house whose lords were known as "iron-masters." The mines are closed now, but we are left with the legacy, the mansion, a lovely state park — and that cyclopean iron chain.

Enough of mystery. The chain was forged at Sterling, a few miles from Ringwood across the New York border, as a means of barring British men-of-war from navigating the Hudson

River beyond West Point. This was a crucial enterprise for the rebels; English control of the Hudson would have effectively cut off New England from New York, and allowed the king's forces free access to the Mohawk Valley, the Great Lakes, and Canada. Four plans had failed by 1778: these had involved "fire ships" — hulks set ablaze after being fastened to enemy vessels; sunken ships mounted with barbs; sixty-foot iron-tipped spears set in sunken timber cribs filled with rocks; and even an earlier Ringwood-forged chain broken by the current because of insufficient size and weight. The last plan had to work, and it did: after the great barrier was floated into place on barges and secured at the opposite shores, no British naval traffic passed West Point for the duration of the war. (No thanks to Benedict Arnold; as part of his planned handover of the Point to the enemy, the famous traitor is said to have agreed to break the chain, but Major Andre, his accomplice, was apprehended in time, and the plan failed.) In 1783, the links were disassembled, and many years afterward the proprietors of Ringwood Manor claimed their share.

The war effort by no means represented the start of the iron industry in the Ramapo region. The first mines near Ringwood were worked as early as 1730; the Ringwood Company itself was organized ten years later. A giant figure in the colonial American mining industry was Peter Hasenclever, a German entrepreneur. When Hasenclever went bankrupt in the years immediately preceding the revolution, management of his Ringwood enterprises passed to Robert Erskine, a Scot who excelled in surveying and cartography as well as mine engineering. He built the first manor house at the Ringwood works, and — having defected to the colonists' cause — oversaw munitions production after hostilities broke out. General Washington, who made his headquarters at the manor during various phases of the New Jersey campaign, named Erskine to the post of Surveyor General of the Continental Army. In this capacity, he drafted many of the earliest reliable maps of the Ramapo Valley and the uplands which surround it. Robert Erskine died in 1780; the path

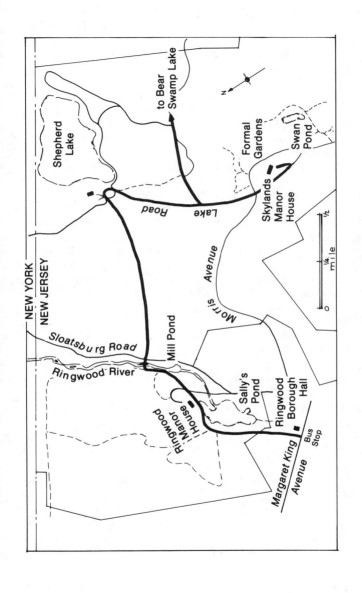

that takes Ringwood visitors from the nearest bus stop to the Manor passes his grave.

PUBLIC TRANSIT: New Jersey Transit serves Ringwood via a route that originates at New York's Port Authority Bus Terminal. Passengers should get off at the Ringwood Borough Hall on Margaret King Avenue. Follow the paved road that begins at the rear of the Borough Hall parking lot and pass (on your left) a white frame building and a gate, at which point the pavement ends.

Continue on the gravel road, which is marked with white blazes with red dots. At about ¼ mile, you will pass through a clearing. Go through the gate at the end of the clearing and bear left. In less than ½ mile, you will come upon a small graveyard (on your right), which contains the remains of Robert Erskine and members of the Hewitt family, last of the ironmasters of Ringwood. Shortly after passing the graveyard, cross a footbridge and bear right to reach the front lawn of Ringwood Manor House.

AUTOMOBILE: Take Interstate 80 to Route 23 North; follow 23 until you reach the exit for Route 511 North to the town of Pompton Lakes. Stay on 511 past Pompton Lakes, with the Wanaque Reservoir on your left. You will see a sign indicating a right turn marked "Ringwood State Park"; the park entrance is 2½ miles from this point. (A parking fee is charged here, as well as at Shepherd Lake and Skylands.)

Having arrived at the park, the first feature likely to attract your interest is the Manor House itself, set handsomely on a knoll behind Sally's Pond. The house you see today is not the small structure put up by Robert Erskine. In fact, only the west wing dates back to the tenancy of the Ryersons, Erskine's successors as masters of the mines and forges, and Peter Cooper, founder of New York's Cooper Union Institute, who purchased the property in 1853. The greater part of the present mansion was built in the late nineteenth century by Abram S. Hewitt, who married Peter Cooper's daughter. The Hewitts were the last private owners of Ringwood Manor; in 1936, Abram's son Erskine gave the house and surrounding lands to the state of New Jersey.

The Manor House at Ringwood, with its gingerbread eaves, broad piazzas, and panelled central hall, retains an informal atmosphere, more squirelike than baronial — especially when compared with Skylands, the neo-Jacobean extravaganza on an adjacent estate. Ringwood predates the age when European castles were the models of domestic architecture for wealthy Americans; as hard as we might find it to imagine living there, it still seems like the abode of people who took their shoes off after dinner, or walked over to the cow barn to talk with the help.

The Manor House is not the only building on park grounds that is open to the public. Opposite the entrance road from the house, and adjacent to the old mill (with its working wooden water wheel), is a gallery exhibiting the work of local artists and craftsmen. A smaller gallery, occupying a wing of the Manor House itself, shows photography, prints, and paintings.

The Ringwood grounds vary, as do the types of recreation they invite: within the immediate vicinity of the Manor House are broad meadows laced with ponds and watercourses, where Canada geese loiter with an eye toward your picnic crumbs; sites equipped with tables and charcoal grills are strung loosely along the loops of the auto road that parallels the Ringwood River. The river itself is stocked annually with trout, while Sally's Pond, near the park entrance, offers pickerel and bass fishing.

THE WALK: A system of walking trails exists allowing short hikes in the immediate area, as well as connections with the farther reaches of park property and other New Jersey state reservations. Since the trail system is fairly elaborate and trail designations and blazing are subject to change, it is recommended that visitors stop at the ranger's office in the east wing of the Manor House for maps — both winter and summer versions are available. (For further

*information, call 201-962-7031.) There are two principal
long-distance (i.e., several hours or more) routes leading
out from the Manor House area. One heads northwest,
toward Abram S. Hewitt State Forest; this is a trip of
approximately six miles one way. The other trail, which
stays largely within the newer, more recent additions to
Ringwood State Park, bridges the Ringwood River just
above the manor's mill pond, crosses Sloatsburg Road, and
traverses a ridge before reaching the southern end of Shepherd Lake, where boating, fishing, and swimming are available. Trail distance from Ringwood Manor House to
Shepherd Lake is about 1½ miles. From the gate at
Shepherd Lake, a 0.8-mile walk along a paved park road
will bring you to the Skylands estate, with its mansion and
formal gardens, acquired by the state of New Jersey in 1967
and now a part of the Ringwood Park holdings. (Skylands
can also be reached by car; the entrance to the estate is 1.4
miles from a marked turnoff on Route 511.)*

As we noted before, Skylands belongs to a different era from the
Manor House at Ringwood: it is a creation of the 1920s, the
Indian summer of the Gilded Age in America. Clarence Mac-
Kenzie Lewis, a New York banker and amateur horticulturist,
built Skylands during the years 1924-1927. Its 44 rooms, including a kitchen-sized chamber used only for the arrangement
of cut flowers, comprised his summer home; winters, he could
be found at 1000 Park Avenue. The tour guide will take you
through the first floor of the mansion, noting Lewis's purchases
of fixtures and furnishings from the great houses of Europe. It is
all quite spectacular (especially the outdoor fireplace on the rear
piazza) but common enough within its time and spirit. What are
truly extraordinary are Lewis's plantings, some of which are
still cultivated as the only botanical garden within the New
Jersey state park system. Although recent budget cuts have
severely reduced the number of horticulturists assigned to main-

taining the gardens, there are still plants in bloom throughout most of the year, and the pathways through the shrubbery and flower beds are always pleasant places to stroll.

From Skylands, trails continue eastward and out of the state's Ringwood property. The easternmost objective for a day user of this trail system would be Bear Swamp Lake, which lies opposite the wooded ridge separating Passaic from Bergen County. The most direct trail from Skylands east to Bear Swamp Lake intersects the Lake Road about halfway between Shepherd Lake and the Skylands mansion; a hiker would turn right onto this trail if coming from the mansion and gardens, left if approaching from the lake. Check with the ranger station at Ringwood Manor for maps and information on recent changes in trail routing and blazes. The total distance from the Lake Road to Bear Swamp Lake is approximately five miles. While a round-trip hike from Ringwood to Bear Swamp Lake and back might be a bit too ambitious for a day's outing — especially if you wish to spend time at Shepherd Lake or the mansion and gardens at Skylands — you might consider spotting a car at the Ramapo Valley Reservation, on Route 202 in Mahwah, NJ, from which Bear Swamp Lake is a 2½-mile westward walk.

BAYARD CUTTING ARBORETUM/ CONNETQUOT RIVER STATE PARK

Walking and (in Connetquot) ski touring — 2 to 13 miles, depending on trails chosen. Arboretum, specializing in coniferous species from throughout the world; park preserve in natural state with many miles of hiking trails.

THERE ARE DAYS WHEN you know you want to go outdoors, but can't decide if you want to take the air in a wild or cultivated natural setting. Down on the south shore of Long Island are two contiguous preserves, the Connetquot River State Park and Bayard Cutting Arboretum, that offer both alternatives. They're both within walking distance of the same two Long Island Railroad stations, so you can postpone your choice until you get off the train. Or, if you get an early start, you'll have time to enjoy both the arboretum and the park.

Although the Bayard Cutting Arboretum has only been open as a public institution since the early 1950s, its magnificent plantings date back a good deal farther. William Bayard Cutting (1850-1912), who started his estate on the Connetquot River in 1878, was a protean character in New York business circles. His grandfather had been a partner of Robert Fulton; the elder Cutting's subsequent cornering of the New York steam ferry monopoly helped launch Bayard's career, but he was very much his own creation nonetheless. He graduated from Columbia Law School at 18, and was admitted to the bar at 21. Branching out from ferries, he began to collect railroad directorships (and one presidency), made his way into banking and insurance, and,

with his brother, founded the American Sugar Beet Company. In the 1870s, Cutting formed his Model Tenement Corporation and built the first Manhattan tenements to feature indoor plumbing. When he reached his middle forties, he went into semi-retirement. He had uses for the time this afforded, as he was a founder of the New York City Opera, Metropolitan Museum of Art, New York Zoological Society, and New York Botanical Gardens; trustee of Columbia University; and vice-president of the New York Chamber of Commerce. In 1886, he built a summer house — the 68-room, half-timbered Tudor mansion that graces the arboretum grounds. From here, Cutting ran the largest dairy on Long Island.

And he planted trees.

Bayard Cutting was a friend of Harvard Professor Charles Sprague Sargent, who served as one of the early directors of Boston's Arnold Arboretum. The two men corresponded frequently, and Sargent presented Cutting with many outstanding tree specimens over the years. Over thirty percent of the mature stock of today's arboretum (discounting naturally occurring trees in outlying portions of the grounds) were gifts of the professor. Sargent also advised the landscape architect who executed the final design of Cutting's estate. His advice must have carried some weight in the horticultural community; the landscape architect's name was Frederick Law Olmstead.

Today, Cutting Arboretum is most famous for its pinetum, or collection of coniferous trees, sadly depleted after the ravages of Hurricane Gloria in 1985, but already in the process of being replanted. Specimens from throughout the world thrive here; this is because, despite the remoteness of their places of origin, they grow naturally in microclimates that resemble conditions on Long Island. Many are the largest individuals of their species on the island. These include an Algerian fir, a blue Spanish fir, and a Sargent weeping hemlock, tortuously sprawling like an enormous bonsai, that is one of the largest trees of its kind in the world. Native species have not been overlooked — just beyond the mansion, along the main drive, stands Long Island's largest

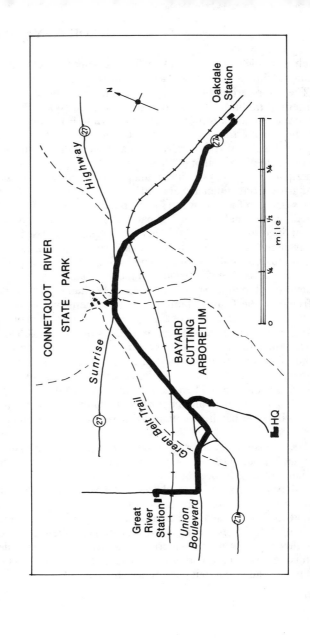

pitch pine, measuring 7 feet, 9 inches at a point 4½ feet from the ground. Rhododendrons and azaleas grow in profusion.

The entire arboretum grounds are a triumph of the English gardening tradition. Unlike the formal French style, the discipline passed down from Capability Brown to F.L. Olmstead is one in which artifice works to reflect a natural, restrained, and organic ideal, rather than striving — as at Versailles — toward a surreal achievement that might as easily have been carved out of marzipan. Water plays an important part; the arboretum stretches along the Connetquot River, and a casual network of streams flows beneath footbridges to meet a pond frequented by swans, ducks, and Canada geese. The paths along the pond were once maintained as moss gardens, but the upkeep of mosses is too labor intensive for the arboretum to keep up the practice.

Although the entire Cutting mansion is not open to the public, there are several exhibit rooms on the first floor. One houses a collection of mounted birds collected by William Henry Trotter, a friend of the Cutting family. The specimens on display are unusual in their freshness of appearance — in most such places, one grows accustomed to seeing feathers uniformly dulled by dust, with here and there a glass eye missing. Look closely at the rather plain little bird labeled "Passenger Pigeon," and then try to imagine the sun blotted from the sky by a million of his like. It wasn't so long ago. There is also an encyclopedic display of eggs, a pair of which are those of the Carolina paraquet. These eggs will never hatch, of course — but neither will any others of that species.

The mansion's former breakfast room (note the glass chip fireplace; Louis Tiffany was another family friend) houses local Indian artifacts. Inspection of the arrowheads on display reveals that they are made of a local quartzite-based rock rather than flint, a material that does not exist in this area. When Long Island Indians wanted flint arrowheads, they bartered for them with upstate tribes, using shell wampum as their currency. Another regional native American idiosyncrasy in this collection is an arrowshaft made from a phragmite reed. These could not have lasted long; but phragmites are plentiful.

BAYARD CUTTING ARBORETUM

.

The Bayard Cutting Arboretum, Oakdale, NY is open Wednesdays through Sundays from 10 AM to 5:30 PM (4:30 PM during Eastern Standard Time). Admission is $1.00, children under 12 free. Although picnicking and active recreation are not permitted, visitors may obtain a transfer pass for nearby Heckscher State Park, where these activities are allowed, at no extra charge.

PUBLIC TRANSIT: Long Island Railroad to Oakdale station (trains more frequent, but a 2-mile walk) or Great River station (½-mile walk). From Oakdale station, turn right onto Main Street (Route 27A). Walk to Sunrise Highway (Route 27) and turn left. Turn left again where Route 27A leaves the Sunrise Highway; arboretum entrance is ahead on your left. From Great River station, walk south (right) 0.2 mile to Union Boulevard; turn left on Union Boulevard and continue until you reach a stop sign. Turn left; arboretum entrance is ahead on your right. The arboretum may also be reached via the S-40 bus, which leaves the Babylon rail station Monday through Saturday.

AUTOMOBILE: Take the Southern State Parkway to exit 45E (Rte. 27A). Head east on 27A approximately ¾ mile to the arboretum entrance. An alternative would be to take Sunrise Highway (Route 27) from the city to Connetquot Avenue and then head south on Connetquot Avenue to Rte. 27A.

THE WALK: There are a number of walks within the 690-acre arboretum property, all of which can be accomplished within a half day's time. These include the Pinetum and Dwarf Evergreen, Wildflower, Rhododendron, Bird Watchers', and Swamp Cypress/Azalea Walks. Maps are available at the Arboretum office in the Cutting mansion.

If you travel to the Cutting Arboretum by way of Great River station, you will notice a crossing marker on Union Boulevard

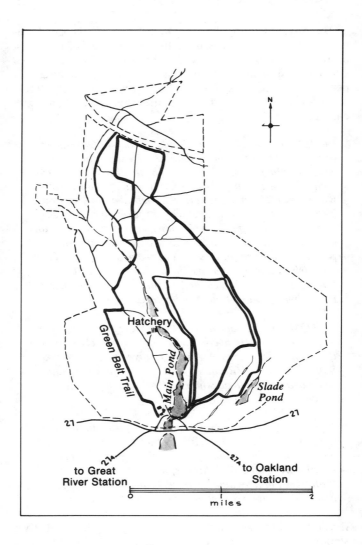

that reads "Green Belt Trail." This is a recently developed north-south route that bisects Long Island from Heckscher State Park to Smithtown. If you turn left onto the trail from Union Boulevard, you will soon reach Sunrise Highway and the entrance to the Connetquot River State Park, New York's first "park preserve."

The history of Connetquot is a long one; fortunately, all of the purposes it has served over the past century and a half were dependent upon its being kept in a natural state. As early as 1836, an establishment called Snedecor's Inn served hunters and fishermen who came seeking the area's abundant game; thirty years later, the place was so popular that a number of its wealthy patrons frequently found it difficult to find rooms. According to a popularly accepted story, these gentlemen decided to remedy the situation by buying Snedecor's and 3,400 adjoining acres. This is how the Southside Sportsmen's Club was formed. The club occupied the old inn buildings and added several others, which still stand near the mill pond at the park's entrance. The rest of the grounds were left undeveloped, as habitat for the fish and game birds that the club raised and released. So things remained for nearly a century, with the club's steady complement of 100 members being the only human beneficiaries of this large parcel of pristine Long Island. Whatever the social arguments might be against exclusive institutions, they have often worked toward the preservation of open lands. Motives are hard to pin down — results are there in black and white.

In 1963, the organization (by then the Connetquot River Club) sold its land to the state, from which it leased occupancy rights until 1973. The park was opened that year, and declared a preserve in 1978.

The status of "preserve" entails certain restrictions on use. There is a $1.00 admission fee to the park, and a permit is required for hiking on all trails except the Green Belt. These may be obtained from the Permit Department, Long Island State Park and Recreation Commission, Babylon, Long Island 11702.

The Commission suggests that trail walkers apply for permits 10 days in advance of planned trips. The procedure is somewhat simpler for cross-country skiing on the trails; skiers may call the park (516-669-1000 or 581-1005) and inform officials of when they plan to arrive. Temporary permits are then issued for that day.

Connetquot is situated in a pine-oak forest on the glacial outwash plain of Long Island's south shore. With the exception of the entranceway and a road leading to the fish hatchery, the only pathways which traverse the preserve are narrow, unpaved fire lanes. These form the trails for walkers; maps are available at the administration building. The park's fauna include blue-birds (note the houses built to attract them), wild turkey, owls, flying squirrels, red fox, and a large deer herd. The deer have evidently long since forgotten the Sportsmen's Club. You cannot penetrate far into the Connetquot woods without encountering at least one or two at perhaps 20 or 30 yards' distance; despite the species' reputation for skittishness, these deer are inclined to saunter away nonchalantly rather than make a mad dash for cover. A bit more patience will be necessary if you wish to see any of the rare bird species nesting at Connetquot — among those sighted to date are osprey, brown creeper, and winter wren. Several uncommon plant species, such as pyxie moss, trailing arbutus, and orchids, can also be found.

PUBLIC TRANSIT: Directions are essentially the same as for Bayard Cutting Arboretum. If you take the Long Island Railroad to Oakdale station, follow Main Street to Sunrise Highway, turn left, and turn right at the next intersection. There is a crosswalk here leading to the park entrance. Sunrise Highway traffic can be heavy, so be careful when crossing. If you came by way of the Great River station, proceed as directed above by way of the Green Belt Trail. From the arboretum entrance, turn right and walk along Route 27A to Sunrise Highway and the park entrance.

BAYARD CUTTING ARBORETUM

AUTOMOBILE: Follow above directions for arboretum, but do not turn right on Route 27A. Make the first permissible U-turn after this intersection, reversing direction on Route 27 and turning right at the park entrance.

THE WALK: Any number of walks are possible, including the white-blazed Green Belt Trail, which runs for 3⅞ miles within the park. Two other trail loops, extending 4⅞ and 8⅜ miles respectively, are also indicated on park maps. Visitors can make reservations for tours guided by park personnel. Many of these walks include visits to the working fish hatchery on the upper Connetquot River. Birding and tree identification walks are also popular. During the appropriate seasons, permits may be secured for fly fishing on the Connetquot, which remains one of Long Island's finest trout streams.

12

PELHAM BAY PARK

*Walking — 4½ miles, including a walk to the Bartow-Pell
mansion. An expansive park on Long Island Sound, occupying
long-settled land with a colorful history. Trail circles one of two
wildlife sanctuaries in the park.*

$\mathbf{B}$ACK AROUND 1970, WHEN an army dressed in surplus
fatigues was fanning out from the cities of the east into the
American hinterland, seeking a place they had heard of where
fruit grew in the winter, a young New Yorker with a minor
medical problem checked in at a hospital emergency room
somewhere in the midwest. In the course of filling out the
necessary forms, the desk nurse asked him where he had been
born. "The Bronx," he answered, his tongue not quite reaching
his teeth as he pronounced "the."

The nurse nodded, and inquired, "Is that spelled like Des
Moines?"

Despite the occasional irresistible anecdote, there is a lot
more to the Bronx than elocutionary lapses. The borough,
which got its name from the seventeenth century farm of Jonas
Bronck, contained some of the earliest settlements in what is
now New York City, even though it was the last part of town to
be thoroughly urbanized. Before the arrival of the Third Avenue
El at 169th Street in 1888, the Bronx was a community of
loosely connected villages, such as those that had grown up
around the Boston Post Road. One of the benefits of delayed
development was that it kept high land values from interfering
with the execution of a masterful park plan. The three crowning

achievements of this plan are Van Cortlandt Park, on the city's northern border; Bronx Park, where the zoo and botanical gardens are located; and Pelham Bay Park, which protrudes into the headwaters of Long Island Sound.

Although Pelham Bay Park today is an open expanse, given over to a golf course, two wildlife refuges, and a public beach, it figured early in the history of colonial settlement. The story of the small communities around the bay reminds us that in the early seventeenth century, relations between east coast settlers and the Indians were by no means predictable.

The stream which defines the western boundary of Pelham Bay Park is called the Hutchinson River. It was named for Anne Hutchinson, a dissenter from the Puritan theocracy of Massachusetts Bay. Having left Boston one step ahead of the pillory — and perhaps the gallows — she settled here with her family and a group of followers. In 1643, however, the entire colony, save for one of Hutchinson's granddaughters, was annihilated in an Indian attack. Around the same time, troubles with the natives led to the abandonment of a peninsula just to the south, which had been settled by John Throgmorton and a band of 30 families. Throgmorton's name survives, however, in the name of the peninsula and the bridge which crosses it: Throg's Neck.

In 1654, some measure of peace was gained by the signing of a treaty between Thomas Pell, an English settler, and the local Indian tribes. Under colonial custom (control of the Bronx, along with New Amsterdam, passed to the British in 1664), Pell and generations of his heirs ruled their holdings as the Lords of Pelham Manor. In 1836, Robert Bartow, a Pell descendant, built the Greek Revival mansion that stands on Shore Road within the present park grounds. This handsome stone house, known as the Bartow-Pell mansion, was purchased by the city in 1888 and since 1915 has served as the headquarters of the International Garden Club. The building and its grounds are open to the public. Call 212-885-1461 for informatin on hours.

The area around the mouth of the Hutchinson River was the scene of a crucial, though little-known, encounter of the Rev-

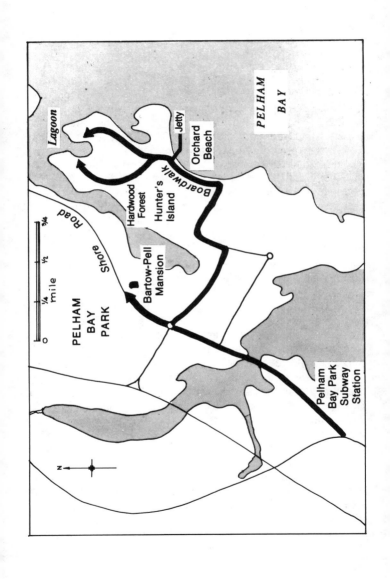

olutionary War. This was the battle of Pell's Point, a classic "holding action" which may very well have prevented the capitulation of a large portion of Washington's army.

On October 12, 1776, General Howe landed at Throg's Neck with a large amphibious force. The Americans were at that time quartered in Harlem Heights; Howe's plan was to cut off any northwest retreat of the Continental Army. This retreat commenced on the 18th of October, with White Plains as its destination. Early that morning, Howe ferried 4,000 troops from Throg's Neck to Pell's Point, where the Hutchinson empties into the Sound. The British general felt that the Point would be a good staging area from which to strike inland at the retreating columns of Americans. This landing was accomplished in secrecy; the regulars and Hessian mercenaries which made up Howe's force penetrated 1½ miles into the interior before colonial spotters saw them. Now, only Colonel John Glover and his four American regiments, totalling a scant 750 men, stood between Howe and his planned rout of Washington's army.

Glover had to think fast. He grouped his men into three detachments, which he deployed at intervals behind the stone walls that lined Split Rock Road. Then Glover sent 40 of his troops out to engage an advance party of 30 British skirmishers. Retreating as they had planned, the Americans lured the British into a hail of fire from the first of the three hidden detachments. This sent the redcoats into a retreat of their own. While they regrouped, the first rank of Americans fell back behind the two fresh regiments, reloaded, and took their places along the walls. This maneuver was repeated several times, with each new advance of the British and Hessians met by fresh volleys from the leapfrogging Continentals. So successful was Glover's ploy that Sir Harry Clinton, commander of the British force, later estimated the number of rebels he had encountered at 14,000. Glover's men, of course, could not hold the enemy back indefinitely; they finally staged a successful retreat to Dobbs Ferry, having suffered casualties of only 6 dead and 13 wounded.

British and Hessian losses were estimated at 200.

This courageous stratagem, along with Howe's hesitation, saved Washington's retreat to White Plains and kept his army from encirclement. Just as important, the story of this exploit raised morale among the Continental troops at a time when their fortunes appeared anything but promising.

The Indians and soldiers are all ghosts now, and Pelham Bay Park is the picture of tranquility. It also presents a markedly different geographical picture than it did prior to this century. The big difference is Hunter's Island, which isn't an island anymore. A narrow channel originally separated what is now Orchard Beach and the Hunter's Island Wildlife Sanctuary from the Bronx mainland. The isolation afforded by this natural moat attracted John Hunter, a New York auctioneer and politician who in 1804 paid $40,000 for the 250-acre island. Hunter built a causeway across the channel, and entertained lavishly at the summer retreat he established on the island. Some of his guests were duly impressed: King Louis Philippe of France even offered — unsuccessfully — to buy the place for his residence-in-exile. The last in the series of owners who followed Hunter sold the island to the city in 1889 for $324,000, which shows that real estate values ballooned just as freely over the course of the past century as they have in our own. Hunter's Island now became part of Pelham Bay Park, and the City, in developing Orchard Beach, filled in what remained of Le Roy's Bay between the island and Pell's Point. Finally, in 1937, Hunter's Georgian mansion was demolished.

PUBLIC TRANSIT: Take the IRT Lexington Avenue Local or Pelham Express to Pelham Bay Park, which is the last stop on the line. From here you can take the No. 12 bus (destination City Island), getting off at Orchard Beach. This bus runs only during peak summer beach times; call New York City transit information (718-330-1234) for schedules. When the bus is not running, walk north from the subway station to Pelham Parkway, cross the causeway, and follow signs for Orchard Beach. This walk of approximately two miles lies entirely within park grounds.

AUTOMOBILE: Take the George Washington Bridge or FDR Drive to the Cross-Bronx Expressway (Interstate 95); take the Cross-Bronx Expressway to Hutchinson River Parkway north and watch for Orchard Beach/City Island signs, then bear right off the Hutchinson and then left for Orchard Beach. An alternate route is FDR Drive to the Third Avenue Bridge, then right onto Bruckner Boulevard and Bruckner Expressway to the Hutchinson River Parkway. From here, proceed as above. (Note: Park gates close at dusk.)

THE WALK: One of the most picturesque walking routes in Pelham Bay Park is the trail that follows the periphery of the Hunter's Island Wildlife Preserve, at the northern end of the peninsula. From the main pavilion at Orchard Beach, follow the boardwalk north to its end at the jetty. From here, starting from the right, you can look out at the northern tip of City Island, Hart Island, Sands Point (on Long Island), Huguenot and David's Islands, and, almost due north, Travers Island. Turn left onto the path that begins just before the end of the boardwalk and continue along any of the paths that wind through the peninsula's northern tip. Turning inland, you will find that the footbridge across the lagoon has become impassable and has been fenced off for safety, so you will have to loop back along the shore to reach the paths that enter the hardwood forest of the Twin Islands Preserve on the other side of the lagoon. The lagoon itself is a good place to pause and watch for waterfowl. Black and white scaup are occasional visitors; snowy egrets are not uncommon.

If you wish to visit the Bartow-Pell mansion, walk inland

PELHAM BAY PARK

from Orchard Beach to the circle, then north (right) along Shore Road. The mansion is on your right. (Total distance from Orchard Beach: approximately 1½ miles.)

13

WATCHUNG RESERVATION

*Walking and ski-touring (trails not groomed) — total distance 8
to 9 miles, including approach from bus stop; 4 to 5 miles
without. Hiking over and between the ridges of New Jersey's
Watchung Mountains, with a stop at an abandoned nineteenth-
century manufacturing village.*

FEW PHYSICAL CONCEPTS are as difficult to deal with as
that of geological time. The geologist makes his peace with the
fathomless eons by naming and telescoping them, as if they
were the hours of a day, although even the most practical student
of the earth's past must realize that his work brings him closer to
the idea of infinity than anyone, save the astronomer or theolo-
gian, is likely to get. For the layman, talk of hundreds of
millions or billions of years will usually produce the same effect
as mention of the federal budget, which — for most of us — is
the only other place where so many zeros can be found. These
numbers bypass circuits in the brain; they exist outside of
comprehension.

Nevertheless, the earth is very old, and it has changed its
shape and structure during many identifiable periods in its long
history. There are few places on the map where evidence of as
many of these distant phases can be found as in the lands
surrounding New York harbor. Nearly every phenomenon
known to geologists has taken place here, including volcanism,
faulting, "folding," metamorphosis, sedimentation, glaciation, and the advance and retreat of primeval seas. The evidence
of all these agents of change is there for the trained eye to read,

and it is accompanied by a remarkable variety of fossils indicating the life forms that found the area habitable during different periods in its development. Some species, of course, leave more grandiose reminders of their sojourn, such as the Pulaski Skyway and the Lackawanna terminal in Hoboken.

We haven't room here to trace all of the slow but relentless processes that created the topography of northern New Jersey. (For a detailed account, see Jerome Wyckoff's *Rock Scenery of the Hudson Highlands and Palisades,* listed in the bibliography at the back of this book.) One particular phase of geological activity, though, is of interest if we are to understand the conspicuous series of ridges that gives the Watchung Reservation its name.

The area between the western New Jersey highlands and the bedrock of Manhattan and the Bronx is known to geologists as the Newark Basin. By the end of the Triassic Period, some 190 million years ago, the principal feature of the basin was a layer of sandstone several thousand feet thick. This sedimentary deposit was the result of erosion in the surrounding mountains; as it lay in the basin, natural forces created cracks and fissures throughout its layers. As molten rock (magma) was thrust upward through the earth's crust during periods of volcanic activity, it found its way into these faults, sometimes breaking the surface, sometimes not. When the magma cooled, it formed rock which was harder and more resistant to erosion than the surrounding sandstone. The millions of years of wind, rain, and inundation which followed the Triassic left the fissure-molded parapets of solidified magma exposed, while the surrounding sedimentary formations receded. Compare a metal casting made in plaster, and not removed from its mold: if left out in the weather, the plaster would eventually disappear, but the metal would remain.

Two major upheavals of molten rock took place in the Newark Basin, leaving two distinct topographical formations. Along what is now the western shore of the Hudson River Valley, the flow of magma penetrated the sandstone rifts but did not break

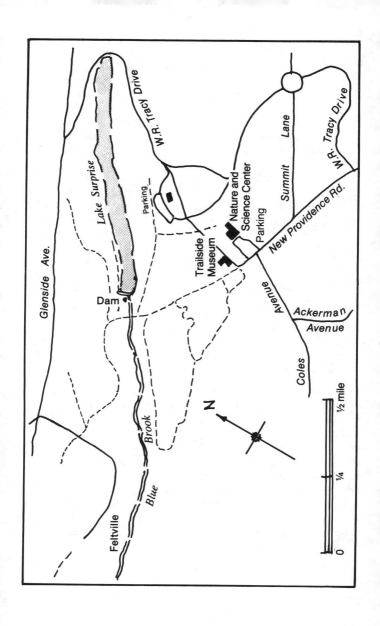

through to the surface; the material cooled slowly, and when erosion had done its work, the Palisades were left to loom above the river. (For a more thorough look at the formation and composition of the Palisades, see Chapter 15.)

Farther to the west, streams of lava with similar mineral components not only coursed through fissures in the sediment, but actually found the surface of the Newark Basin. This material cooled rapidly into the hard, close-grained rock that we know today as basalt. The basalt formations of northern New Jersey had yet to attain their vertical prominence in the terrain; in fact, they were even covered for a time by later deposits of sediment. Their elevation came about not only as a result of erosion but because of shifts in the earth's crust, which raised the hardened magma above its sedimentary environment. The finished products — or, at least, the products that we see at our stage in geological time — are the Watchung Mountains, two parallel north-south ridges generally designated "First" and "Second," which hook sharply to the west at their northern and southern extremes. The name "Watchung" comes from the Lenni Lenape "Wach Unks," meaning high hills.

New Jersey could never have played the part it did in the American Revolution if it were not for the natural fortification that the Watchungs offered to the Continental Army (see Chapter 7). George Washington's strategic retreats across the state are legendary, but it is no slight to the commander's military genius to suggest that the Watchungs made these maneuvers — and the defense of his headquarters at Morristown — a good deal easier than they otherwise might have been. Even today, the range offers a barrier of sorts: east of the Watchungs lies industrial New Jersey, while to the west, the landscape is decidedly suburban, even rural. Whether things will remain this way, now that the interstate highway system has succeeded where the British failed, is anyone's guess. Meanwhile, we should be appreciative of the efforts that led to preserves such as the Watchung Reservation.

WATCHUNG RESERVATION

*PUBLIC TRANSIT: The Watchung Reservation lies be-
tween Summit, to the north, and Scotch Plains, to the south.
Although NJ Transit commuter trains run from Hoboken to
Summit and several other surrounding communities, none
of the stations are within reasonable walking distance of the
reservation. The best alternative is to take any of the buses
from Newark or New York that travel along Route 22
toward Scotch Plains and North Plainfield. Get off at New
Providence Road, just past Mountainside. Walk uphill on
New Providence Road to W.R. Tracy Drive, where you will
see a reservation sign. Turn right onto Tracy Drive; when
you reach a circle, bear left to reach the Trailside Museum.
Or, you can walk farther on New Providence Road, past the
point where it turns toward the left, then turn right onto
Deer Path, right again onto Ackerman Avenue, and then
right onto Coles Avenue, which will take you to the reservation's Nature and Science Center. The first route is approximately two miles; the second is a bit shorter. Both take you
along tree-lined roads through pleasant neighborhoods.*

*AUTOMOBILE: Take the New Jersey Turnpike or Garden
State Parkway to Route 22 west. Take the Mountainside/
New Providence Road exit and proceed uphill (north). Turn
right onto Tracy Drive and take the third exit out of the
traffic circle. When the road turns sharply left, turn right to
reach the Nature and Science Center parking lot.*

The Watchung Reservation is maintained by the County of
Union, Department of Parks and Recreation. Although there is a
service pavilion, broad central lawn, and some cultivated planting (rhododendrons bloom in late spring), most of the nearly
2,000 acres of the reservation have been preserved in their
original wild and wooded state. Hiking and bridle trails traverse
most of the tract; maps are available at the Trailside Nature and
Science Center. A special feature is the 10-mile Sierra Club

Trail, which makes a rough peripheral circuit within the boundaries of the reservation.

The principal developed facilities at Watchung are the Trailside Museum, which contains a thorough exhibit of indigenous or once-indigenous species of birds and mammals, as well as birds' eggs, and the newer Nature and Science Center, offering, in addition to its permanent collections, films, lectures, workshops, and planetarium shows. Schedules are available from the Center, Coles Avenue and New Providence Road, Mountainside, NJ 07092 (201-232-5930).

THE WALK: There are four color-coded nature trails within the reservation, maps of which are available at the Nature and Science Center. In addition to these trails and the peripheral Sierra Club Trail, paths (also indicated on reservation maps) lead from the Nature Center and Museum to Surprise Lake and the deserted village of Feltville.

Feltville isn't completely deserted; a couple of the houses are occupied. Vandalism and arson being what they are nowadays, either a village is partly occupied or it ceases to exist. But this little group of wooden structures has a spectral feeling nonetheless. There had been a saw and grist mill here for some years before 1845, when David Felt, a New York City businessman, selected it as a site for a paper-manufacturing and printing business — an early attempt at vertical integration. Buildings went up, workers moved in, and the place prospered until 1860, at which time Felt lost interest and moved away. By 1880 it was a ghost town. (To learn more about the village, see the Feltville exhibit at the Nature and Science Center.)

For an interesting walk that takes you beyond the deserted village, walk past the road's end (white wooden structure on left) and follow the white markers of the Sierra Trail. The trail soon gets much narrower; at this point, you begin to get a good sense of being in a valley between the two

Watchung Mountains. At ¾ mile past the village, the trail crosses an unbridged stream, which can be forded with dry feet if you step carefully on the rocks. During spring runoff, there may be more of a problem. Less than 100 yards uphill from the stream is a T intersection. Unless you wish to follow the white markers and stay on the longer Sierra Trail, which leads to the old Drake Farm, bear left here, keeping the stream to your right. Turn left again at the next T intersection. Not far from here, on the left, is small, nearly overgrown Hermit's Pond, bounded at the opposite end by a crumbling brick retaining wall and culvert. An abundance of wild watercress grows here in season. This is a miniature but instructive example of the way aquatic vegetation constitutes the first step in the succession from pond, to bog, to dry land.

To return, get back on the main trail that passes by the pond and continue downhill to the trail that parallels Blue Brook. Cross the bridge to get back onto the Blue Trail leading back toward the Museum and Nature and Science Center. (Use of reservation map is recommended.)

14

CLOISTERS/INWOOD HILL PARK

*Walking — 4½ miles. A visit to the Cloisters, followed by a
downhill-and-up-again walk along one of Manhattan's most
prominent rock ridges. Turnaround point is Spuyten Duyvil
Creek, which separates Manhattan from the Bronx.*

ART AND NATURE ARE all there is to life, and this walk has
them both. It also follows an unusual route, taking us to the
northern tip of Manhattan Island by way of the Middle Ages.

The Cloisters is the Metropolitan Museum's repository of
medieval art. It occupies an enviable and commanding position
on the wooded heights of Fort Tryon Park, near the George
Washington Bridge, and derives its name from the deliberate-
ness with which its designers set about reproducing the appearance and atmosphere of a twelfth-century monastery. Although
no one structure served as a model for this New York anachron-
ism, the Cloisters was inspired by the priory of San Michel de
Cuxa in the French Pyrenees.

Parts of the Cloisters are indeed ancient. These rooms, columns, and courtyard fragments have been carefully incorporated into the building, although each is identified so that the
visitor does not confuse original and reproduction segments of
the same architectural units. The apse from the 1160 church of
San Martin in Funtiduena, Segovia, however, is entirely original, having been dismantled and transported stone by stone to
New York. It is on indefinite loan from the Spanish government, which one hopes takes the long view in defining "indefinite."

The history of the Cloisters dates to 1926, when John D. Rockefeller, Jr. donated funds to the Metropolitan to purchase the medieval sculpture collection of George Grey Bernard, an American sculptor. Rockefeller added relevant pieces from his own trove of pre-Renaissance art, and in 1930 deeded to the Met the land that comprises Fort Tryon Park, where the museum now stands.

The treasures of the Cloisters are well catalogued and described in museum publications as well as in unofficial guides. However, we might mention a few of the collection's highlights, such as the Romanesque ivory cross of Bury St. Edmonds, carved with 108 figures and 60 inscriptions; the Antioch chalice, one of the Cloisters' earliest examples of Christian art, once thought to be the Holy Grail; and two matchless illuminated devotional volumes — *Les Belles Heures* of Jean, Duke of Berry, and the *Hours* of Jeanne d'Evreux. But perhaps the best known of all the Cloisters' holdings are the Unicorn tapestries. These richly detailed allegorical textiles were woven in France just prior to the turn of the sixteenth century. Viewed in sequence, they tell of the capture of the mythical unicorn, but their pictorial quality is every bit as fascinating as their narrative purpose. The flowers blooming in the fields of these tapestries are so bright, so alive, that one almost sniffs as well as looks at them. There is nothing but art and nature, and in this room they are in very close proximity.

The two come together on a larger scale just outdoors, where the terraces of the Cloisters meet the steep slope of Fort Tryon Park. Here are the museum's medieval herb gardens and espaliered fruit trees, along with splendid views of the Hudson, its Palisades, and — shall we count great engineering as art? — the George Washington Bridge. This is where to begin the walk that reaches, within less than two miles, the point at which Manhattan runs out of land.

PUBLIC TRANSIT: To get to Fort Tryon Park, take either

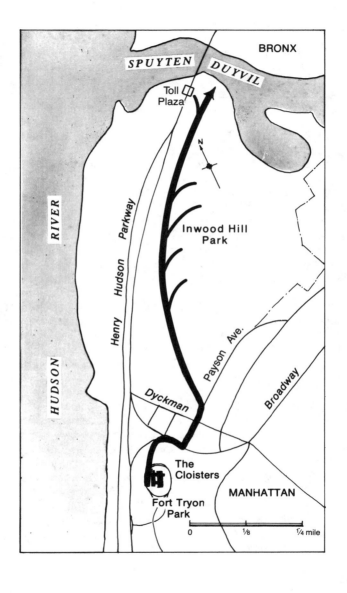

BRONX

SPUYTEN DUYVIL

Toll Plaza

N

RIVER

Henry Hudson Parkway

Inwood Hill Park

Payson Ave.

Broadway

HUDSON

Dyckman

The Cloisters

MANHATTAN

Fort Tryon Park

0   1/8   1/4 mile

the Madison Avenue bus No. 4, or the IND 8th Avenue A train to the 190th Street station.

AUTOMOBILE: Take the Henry Hudson Parkway north to exit 8; follow signs for Cloisters.

Fort Tryon Park occupies much of the highest ground in Manhattan — the actual "summit" of the island is close by, near the intersection of 183rd Street and Fort Washington Avenue. Naturally, this prominence gave the area strategic importance during the American Revolution. The colonial installation here was called Fort Washington. On the 16th of November, 1776, rebel forces lost the fort to a numerically superior force of British and Hessians. The RMS *Pearl*, at anchor in the Hudson, cut off that avenue of retreat, and 2,600 Americans were taken prisoner. This set the stage for the successful British attack on Fort Lee, on the New Jersey side (see Chapter 15), and marked the loss of New York for the remainder of the war. It is ironic, then, that the George Washington Bridge, one of the most impressive of the monuments to be named after the general, should be anchored on either bank near the sites of engagements that he might just as well not have cared to recall.

THE WALK: Follow the pathway that begins at the rear (river side) of the Cloisters, heading downhill with the Hudson to your left. As you near the bottom of the hill, take a sharp left turn to reach the Payson Avenue exit of Fort Tryon Park. (If you continue straight at this point, you will come out of the park on Broadway.) Walk down Payson Avenue to Dyckman Street. As you cross Dyckman Street, you will notice a playground on your left. Just past the playground a broad, paved pathway leads into Inwood Hill Park. Turn left here, heading uphill, and bear left at the next path intersection. When you emerge into a small paved clearing, bear left again onto the main path leading north toward Inwood Hill and the tip of the island.

In walking downhill from the Cloisters, through the city streets, and back onto higher ground, you are traversing a geological feature called the "Dyckman Street gap." This is an east-west break in the ridge of Manhattan schist that runs the length of the island, and thus serves as the foundation for the city's tall buildings. Manhattan schist is one of three metamorphic strata — the other two being Fordham gneiss and Inwood dolomite — that form the bulk of the bedrock formation known as the "Manhattan Prong." A ridge of dolomite also begins an upward thrust around Dyckman Street, and becomes visible in the limestone face along the Spuyten Duyvil's Bronx shore. But it is essentially the Paleozoic Manhattan schist that gives Inwood Hill Park its muscular profile, and also defines the bastions of Fort Tryon Park and Washington Heights before sloping southwards toward sea level.

Inwood Hill Park is the most northerly part of Manhattan, and it is also the loneliest and most remote. It is easy to see that Central Park was left open by design — it is surrounded on all sides by buildings, and the landscaping, however artless and informal, is still identifiable as a conscious effort. But Inwood is different. One senses that these huge trees and rough outcroppings of stone were left untouched because this is where the great machine that pushed itself north from the Battery finally lost momentum — that having come this far, the city said "enough." Well, the simple fact of the Bronx may belie such an impression; but Inwood looks like wilderness still. It is a throwback to a time before the Unicorn tapestries were woven, when Indians shucked oysters in the rock caves along the Spuyten Duyvil.

Inwood Hill Park is not completely wild. Its mature hardwood forest is threaded with walkways, along which can be seen evidence of a barbarism much worse, in its way, than that which the Indians represented to the first white settlers. When this land was set aside as a park, the paths were illuminated with sturdy, globe-topped cast iron lamps. Today, if you look long and hard, you might find one with its globe still intact. You won't have to

look hard at all to find places where the cast iron posts themselves have been broken. The Indians, whatever other uncivil-
ized traits they may have possessed, did not raise their children
to destroy the things that belonged to the tribe.

*To reach the tip of the island, continue uphill, keeping the
sound of traffic on the Henry Hudson Parkway to your left.
Head straight over Inwood Hill on the paved path. (If you
take any of the right-hand turnoffs onto narrower paths,
just remember to keep the traffic sounds to your left and
you'll eventually reach Spuyten Duyvil.) At the point where
the paved path veers left toward the Henry Hudson Parkway toll plaza, bear right onto a dirt path and head down to
Spuyten Duyvil. This narrow channel, which connects the
Harlem River with the Hudson and separates Manhattan
from the Bronx, is shown on some early maps as "Spike and
Devil," apparently for no other reason than the British
penchant for anglicizing and phoneticizing foreign names.*

While you walk, see if you can spot one of the park's black
squirrels. These are grey squirrels possessing a genetic trait
called melanism, which is passed along through generations of
the species living in closed communities such as the one in the
park.

*Return by reversing direction on the path system, eventu-
ally reaching public transportation at Broadway, or, if you
have parked your car at the Cloisters, crossing Dyckman
Street and re-entering Fort Tryon Park. (Approximately
4½ miles, including return to Cloisters.)*

15

THE PALISADES

Walking — up to 10 miles. Trail along the base of the traprock cliffs that line the New Jersey shore of the Hudson north of the George Washington Bridge, with paths connecting with the Long Path on the top of the 400-foot traprock formations.

NOT ALL FJORDS ARE in Scandinavia, or along the coasts of Alaska and British Columbia. They are scarce, though, on the eastern seaboard of the United States. Somes Sound, in Maine, is one; the other is the Hudson River Valley.

The old Hudson, a fjord? It isn't as exotic as it sounds. A fjord is simply a riverbed that has been gouged deeper than sea level by a glacier, and later filled with its meltwater. There you have the Hudson: it is a drowned, tidal river, with scarcely a five-foot drop between Albany and New York harbor. It is only the current of the stream, fed by the melting snows of the Adirondacks, that prevents salt water from reaching even farther than Marlborough, just south of Poughkeepsie. Tides affect the river as far north as Troy.

But the Hudson does have something (aside from New York City) that sets it apart. These are the towering cliffs of the Palisades, which extend over 40 miles along the New Jersey and New York shorelines from the point where they first become visible, to High Tor, where they taper into insignificance.

The glacier left its scars upon the Palisades, but it was not responsible for their formation. In an earlier chapter on New Jersey's Watchung Reservation, we noted that the range of basalt hills which bears that name is the product of an eruption of

molten rock into fissures in the sandstone of the Newark Basin, some 190 million years ago, followed by the erosion of the sediment and revealing of the hardened lava. The Palisades had a similar beginning, with one important difference: while the Watchung upheaval broke the surface, the flow that created the more easterly formation did not. This resulted in a longer cooling time for the Palisades rock, a phenomenon which is revealed by the nature of its crystals. The exposed, fast-cooling Watchung basalt has a dense texture in which little mineral crystallization can be noticed. The rock of the Palisades, called *diabase*, contains coarser, visible crystals of feldspar and pyroxene.

Another readily noticeable characteristic caused by the underground cooling of the Palisades is the columnar, prism-like structure of the cliffs. This is the result of the contraction and vertical splintering that took place as the rock solidified. To the Indians, these columns had an organic appearance — thus their word for them, which remains as the name of a nearby New Jersey town: *Wee-awk-en*, the rocks that look like trees. Our word for the cliffs comes from the old military term "palisade," which was an enclosure made up of sharpened stakes driven into the ground. The French verb *paliser*, meaning "to enclose with pales," is at the root of all this.

Despite the suggestion of impregnability in this etymology, the Palisades did not prove to be the most readily defensible local natural feature for the colonists in the Revolutionary War. After the British overran Manhattan's Fort Washington (see Chapter 14), their next logical step was to cross the Hudson and attack Fort Lee, a ¼-acre, four-sided citadel occupying a site now within the town of the same name. They commenced their assault by firing on Fort Lee with cannon captured from Fort Washington; the American commander, who was with his men on the Jersey side, thus suffered the indignity of being shot at with artillery from his namesake fort. All irony aside, try to imagine the spectacle of cannonballs flying in both directions

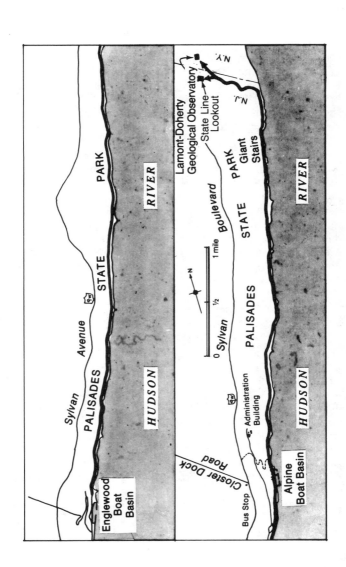

across the river where the bridge now stands, while acrid smoke trailed into the November sky.

Washington and his troops had no time for such reflection. Lord Cornwallis and a contingent of British and Hessians were landing just upriver at Alpine; Fort Lee was abandoned with such alacrity that kettles were left simmering on its fires. The great retreat across New Jersey had begun. It would be five years before the Union Jack was struck from Fort Lee.

As befits their reputation, the men of the nineteenth century looked across to the Palisades and saw not trees (although they harvested the real ones), not fortifications, but rock. With a project like New York City underway, rock came in handy. The hard diabase was useful for any number of things, one of the most important of which was asphalt paving. Quarries opened at the base of the cliffs and thrived upon their steady depletion. Meanwhile, the New Jersey bank of the Hudson, south of present-day Edgewater, was beginning to resemble its cross-river counterpart more and more. If you visit Union City, Weehawken, or Hoboken today, the only indication of the area's vertical topography is the descending, step-like appearance of factory and warehouse roofs.

By the 1890s, many citizens had begun to wonder if the Palisades were doomed — and what, if anything, could be done about it. Attempts to get the government to buy the cliffs for use as a military reservation came to naught. Finally, under pressure from the New Jersey Federation of Women's Clubs, the governor of that state appointed a committee to look into acquisition of the Palisades for park development. The New Jersey committee worked with a similar group from New York, which had been organized by American Scientific and Historic Preservation Society head Andrew Green under directives from Governor Theodore Roosevelt. The bi-state panel soon recommended purchase of the endangered cliffs to the New York and New Jersey legislatures. No plans for acquisition of the land at the top of the cliffs were made, largely because most people thought that this plateau would remain inaccessible to development.

THE PALISADES

Fortunately, this misjudgement was later rectified; had it not been, the high-rises of Fort Lee might well have marched to the New York border.

The next step was the formal establishment of a joint commission, empowered and funded by both legislatures to buy park land. New York put in $10,000, New Jersey $5,000. Even in those days that was hardly enough money — though most landowners were willing to sell property at the cliff base for between $200 and $500 per acre, with $10 per foot for riparian rights, purchase of the quarries themselves was a more expensive proposition. The most destructive single operation could be had for $132,500. The commission received an option to buy in return for the $10,000 grant from New York state, and began to search for additional funds.

They didn't search long. George Perkins, the commission's president, was a business partner of J. P. Morgan. Morgan must have been in a good mood when he was approached about the project, because Perkins went away with the great banker's check for $122,500. The blasting of the Palisades stopped on Christmas Eve, 1900.

The rest of the lands that now make up Palisades Interstate Park were assembled piecemeal over the next 10 years, with the dedication taking place on September 27, 1909. Not all of the many parcels that made up the park had been in the hands of quarrying concerns or estate holders. In colonial times, a settlement called "Under the Mountain" had grown up in the shadow of the cliffs, and descendants of the community's farm families lingered at the spot as recently as the beginning of our own century. A small graveyard, near the Englewood Boat Basin, commemorates these inhabitants of one of the most unusual pieces of real estate in the metropolitan area.

What is most unusual about the Palisades today, though, is the contrast they offer to everything that surrounds them. Nowhere else is it possible to feel at once so close to the great city and yet so far from it; when the day is clear and the skyline sharp, the stony heights of Manhattan seem themselves like great silent cliffs, and the tumult below them becomes very hard to imagine. For the walker, the sense of isolation which the Palisades afford is most pronounced along the Shore Path, with the Hudson at one hand and the rocks-that-look-like-trees at the other. The Long Path, which runs along the crest of the formation, is unquestionably scenic, but the views of the cliffs are more spectacular from below. A greater variety of terrain also presents itself to the shoreline walker — in some places the trail runs right along the water, while in others it slabs inland along the lesser grades that rise toward the vertical. Near the New York state line, the Shore Path traverses a jumble of enormous boulders called the Giant Stairs.

PUBLIC TRANSIT: To Englewood Boat Basin/Shore Path: From the Port Authority's uptown terminal near the Manhattan entrance to the George Washington Bridge, take the No. 9 or 9A Red and Tan Lines bus that heads north on Route 9W. Get off at Palisades Avenue in Englewood Cliffs, New Jersey and follow either the auto road or pedestrian path down to the boat basin.

AUTOMOBILE: Take the George Washington Bridge to New Jersey and exit onto 9W north. Take 9W to Palisades Avenue and proceed as above. Parking is available at the boat basin. Depending on your destination, you may wish to spot another car at a point farther north — at the Alpine Boat Basin, State Line Lookout, or Lamont-Doherty Observatory (see below).

THE WALK: The Shore Path is marked with white blazes. Head north along the river from the boat basin; the extent of your walk will be determined by whether you decide to backtrack to Englewood from a selected point, or head for one of the connector trails that extend uphill at gaps in the cliffs. If you choose the latter course and haven't spotted a car, you can return on foot via the Long Trail, or take a

southbound bus along Route 9W.

One possible destination is the Alpine Boat Basin (approximately 5½ miles distant from Englewood), where a trail branches off through a series of switchbacks to the crest. Here it joins the Long Path. To your right, about ¼ mile distant, is the park's administration building; to your left is a road that loops south toward the intersection of Route 9W and Closter Dock Road. This is where the bus to New York stops.

More ambitious hikers can continue past the Alpine Boat Basin on the Shore Path to the New Jersey-New York state line (not marked). At the boat basin, you'll see the small white clapboard house that served as Cornwallis's headquarters after he crossed the Hudson from New York. It was here that the Palisades Interstate Park was dedicated in 1909. From here, the white blazes take you along a broad path set back from the river on higher ground (though a number of trails lead down to water level). About ½ mile beyond the boat basin, look for a white arrow painted on a rock. Go right to stay on the Shore Path, left to head up to the Long Path.

If you choose to continue along the Shore Path, you will soon reach the monumental rockfall known as the Giant Stairs. The white blazes continue through the rocks, which go on for several hundred yards and require fairly nimble footwork — no technical expertise is necessary, but good sneakers or hiking boots are a must.

Finally, when the rock scrambling is over, the trail drops down toward the shore again and begins a series of switchbacks leading to the top of the cliffs. At the top, the white-blazed trail meets a blue-blazed trail, which descends from the left down a log and stone stairway. Climb the stairs and follow the trail to the State Line Lookout, a possible car-spotting place (one problem: there is a two-hour parking limit posted here). Or, passing the stairs, you can follow a poorly marked trail leading to the parking lot of Columbia University's Lamont-Doherty Geological Observatory on the New Jersey-New York state line. The No. 9 and 9A Red and Tan buses stop across from the observatory's entrance on Route 9W. As for parking, it is tacitly permitted on weekdays but a sticker is required at night and on weekends. There is some room for parking outside the gates, however.

Should you walk along the riverbank until you reach the stone ruins of a formal garden, at the base of a falling stream, you will have passed the spur to the Long Path, although a rough, unblazed trail makes the ascent here to the observatory grounds. The garden structures, incidentally, were part of "Cliffside," the estate of Mrs. Lydia G. Lawrence, one of the major land donors to the original Palisades Park Commission. (Total distance from Englewood Boat Basin to observatory is approximately 10 miles.)

16

FORT TILDEN

Walking — 2 to 6 miles. A largely man-made dune environment with a military past. Location on Atlantic flyway makes for good birding during migration seasons.

IN THE 1980s, we have come to think of "defense" as an amorphous commodity, provided by a globe-ranging armada of bombers and submarines, and by intercontinental missiles bristling beneath prairies far from the centers of our national life. But we have only just left the era that began with the first crude village fence, and that included among its defense paraphernalia the city wall, the crenellated tower, and — more recently — the 16-inch gun. This was an era in which defense was localized, and the enemy kept from one's door by the armaments deployed on one's threshold. Fort Tilden, near the western tip of the Rockaway peninsula, is a reminder that this era ended for New York only within the past decade.

Fort Tilden is one among several decommissioned military posts incorporated into the Gateway National Recreation Area since that park's creation in 1973. Government administration of the peninsular site dates to 1812, shortly after which the Rockaway Point Life Saving Station was established. It was finally commissioned as a fort early in 1917; in the beginning, it was known as Fort Funston, in honor of a hero of the Mexican border wars of that era. The present name was chosen later in 1917 as a tribute to Samuel J. Tilden, late governor of New York and one-time Democratic presidential nominee. Although the fort saw no action in World War I, it was modernized in the

years immediately following. As artillery technology advanced, mortars were replaced with 6- and 12-inch guns, which gave way in turn to 16-inch giants capable of firing a projectile weighing as much as an automobile over a distance of 30 miles. The last conventional gun emplacements had a bore diameter of 90 mm. These were supplanted, beginning in 1954, with the Nike-Hercules missile system, but this phase of our coastal defense lasted less than 20 years. The fort was decommissioned in 1974.

What has all this military history to do with a walk on the beach? The answer is simply that it would have been a very different beach, in both topographical and ecological terms, had the fort not existed. The Rockaway peninsula is part of the barrier beach that defines Long Island's south shore. At the time Fort Tilden was commissioned, the dune formations characteristic of this environment extended only a brief way inland. The remainder of the present Breezy Point/Fort Tilden area consisted of salt marsh, which made poor footing for heavy gun emplacements and military vehicle traffic. Landfill was carted to the fort continuously between the years 1911 and 1930, and in 1938, with war looming, a second major land-building effort began.

The fill project was partly intended to give the land stability, but another reason was the concealment of artillery positions. To the untrained eye, one dune looks much like another at Fort Tilden. But only the primary dunes here are the result of natural wind and tidal processes. Secondary dunes — those arrayed just inland from the front, sea-facing rank — are usually a natural phenomenon, resulting from the landward creep of primary dunes and their eventual front-line replacement. Not so on this stretch of beach: some of the inner dunes were built to hide the guns themselves, some to camouflage command bunkers, and some to provide a vantage for spotters who kept gunners apprised of hits and misses during practice firing. No dune will survive without some anchoring vegetation, so the army planted 250,000 trees at Fort Tilden, many of which still survive. Pitch

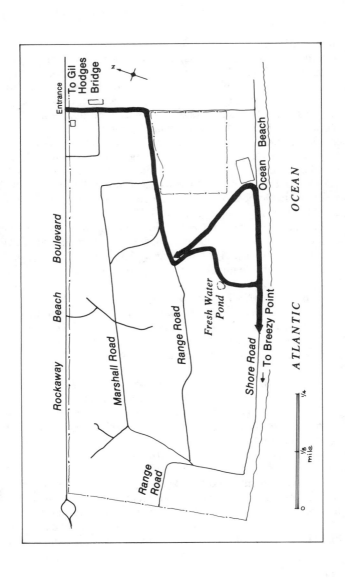

pine and poplar are the most common species. Russian and autumn olive also thrive along the dune paths. Their fruit, along with the abandoned fort's generally dense scrub forestation, assures an abundant population of birds, especially during spring and fall migrations. In reclaimed as well as wilderness settings, the presence of one species leads to that of another. Yellow-rumped warblers, for example, appear by the thousands at migration time. They are a convenient meal for sharp-shinned hawks, and even for kestrels, whose diet is more often confined to insects despite their popular name of "sparrowhawk." Hawk-banding crews go to work each fall at the fort. On one weekend in October of 1979, their count was between 1,200 and 1,500 raptors sighted, and 92 banded.

The land occupied by Fort Tilden — and now by what is called the Breezy Point Unit of Gateway — is hardly the tidal marsh it once was. But a new ecosystem has taken hold, and continues to thrive under the park's careful management.

PUBLIC TRANSIT: Take the IND A (8th Avenue Express) or CC (8th Avenue Local) to the end of the line at Rockaway Park/Beach 116th Street. From here, take the Green bus line to the Gateway Fort Tilden entrance. The same bus serves Jacob Riis Park, now also a Gateway facility.

AUTOMOBILE: Take the Belt Parkway to exit 11-S, then south across the Gil Hodges Bridge to Beach Channel Drive. Turn right onto Beach Channel Drive; the fort entrance is just ahead on your left. A parking permit is required, and may be secured on the day of entry at the unit headquarters just inside the entrance on your left.

Trail development at Fort Tilden has proceeded in conjunction with plans for the restoration and interpretation of some of the former military facilities, and with concern for the maintenance of the delicate dune environment. Officials would like to refurbish at least one of the old Nike missile silos for inclusion on

guided tours, and the offices in the main command bunker —
entirely concealed beneath a man-made dune — will eventually
open as a museum.

*THE WALK: Depending upon individual interest, you may
either include or ignore the military aspects of Fort Tilden
in your walk. Many of the installations were made to be
unobtrusive; time and nature are rendering them more so.
A trail has been laid out that will take walkers from the
administration buildings at the entrance, along the range
road, and onto pathways leading toward the secondary and
primary dune formations and the ocean beach. Once at the
oceanfront, you may turn right and follow the shore road
(now used largely for fishing access) to the tip of
Breezy Point. Trail information is available at the unit
headquarters near the entrance, as are details on special
tours and programs, which are scheduled throughout the
summer. All trail walkers are urged not to cross the dunes
directly in order to get to the ocean beach, as walking on
loose sand and anchor plants increases the risk of erosion.
If you find yourself off a marked trail, use only natural
"blowthroughs" for passing between dunes to the beach.*

17

GREAT SWAMP

Walking — several miles of wilderness trails, with a one-mile observation boardwalk planned. A vast virgin wetland in north central New Jersey, much of it protected under federal wilderness legislation, unparalleled in the area for the birding and botanical study opportunities it offers.

ABOUT FIVE MILES SOUTHWEST of Paterson, New Jersey, there is a gap in the Watchung Mountains through which the Passaic River flows. The place, and the town around it, are called Little Falls; this distinguishes the cataract there from the much larger torrent downriver at Paterson. Little though these falls may be, it is here that the story of the Great Swamp begins — or, conversely, where the story of Lake Passaic ends.

Lake Passaic? Passaic is a county, a city, a river, a township down by Bernardsville — but where is the lake? Not anywhere; not today. But 10,000 years ago, the retreating Wisconsin Ice Sheet had both blocked all channels leading through the Watchungs to the sea, and melted sufficiently to fill the resulting basin with up to 200 feet of water. This was Lake Passaic. It was far bigger than any modern-day New Jersey lake, ranging up to 30 miles in length and 10 miles in width. But the glacier that created it was also its undoing. When the retreating ice mass uncovered the gap at Little Falls, the cork was pulled: what had been a lake became instead a vast wetland, its substratum consisting of clay deposited there by the glacial meltwater streams of the past centuries. Since dense clay drains poorly, the water table of the old lake bed remained right on the surface,

permeating layers of peat and muck. Swamp conditions persisted over much of north-central Jersey.

The human assault on this enormous sponge has been thorough and unrelenting, but vestiges remain. There is Big Piece Meadow in Caldwell and Fairfield; Hatfield Swamp along the Passaic in Roseland; and, farther south, the largest remnant of all: the Great Swamp. It is the domain of wood ducks and bog turtles, red foxes and gallinules, pickerel frogs and opossums.

A swamp ought to be a peaceful enough place, despite the life-and-death struggles constantly waged by those of its denizens who occupy the so-called lower orders. But in recent years, the putatively sentient creatures who live around the Great Swamp have made it a symbolic battlefield over which two weighty issues have been contested. The first of these concerned the very survival of the swamp and was happily resolved. The second has to do with the individual members of the deer population, rather than the species' overall habitat, and it appears to defy settlement.

By 1959, it had occurred to the master planners of the Port Authority of New York and New Jersey that metropolitan air traffic would increase beyond the capacities of Idlewild (later Kennedy), La Guardia, and Newark Airports, and that yet another facility was needed. They consulted their maps and came up with the Great Swamp. (Later, the Pine Barrens would attract their attention, although these too have been saved.) The people who lived around the swamp may not previously have thought much about it, except as a staging area for parties of garbage-raiding raccoons, but the jetport plan made them take another look. The prospect of takeoff and landing noise intruding upon the quiet of one of New Jersey's most desirable residential areas surely had something to do with the ensuing outcry, but an awakened awareness of the swamp's ecological importance must also be credited. Besides, why quibble over motivation? If the creatures who live in the swamp could pause to reflect, it is doubtful whether they would care whether their

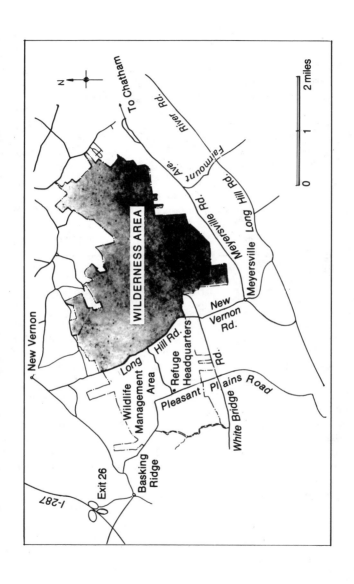

salvation was owed to worries over property values or a concern for wetlands preservation.

The battle was joined, and the battle was won. Local citizens formed the Great Swamp Committee, and, with the enthusiasm of volunteers in a presidential campaign, they beat the bushes for money with which to purchase the bulk of the swamp property and donate it to the U.S. Department of the Interior. The first tract acquired totaled 3,000 acres; this formed the core of the new refuge, which was officially dedicated in 1964. Since then, 3,000 more acres have been added through direct government purchase. Interior now controls 80 percent of the swamp; as of this writing, plans are under way for the acquisition of an additional 1,200 acres on the southwestern borders of the refuge. Most of the new acreage will be devoted to public recreational uses such as hiking and canoeing and to interpretational programs, thus taking pressure off the wildlife management and wilderness areas within the preserve.

The word "wilderness" here carries a political as well as ecological definition. In 1968, the eastern two-thirds of the swamp became the first wilderness area to be located within a National Wildlife Refuge. As such, the 3,600 acres within the specified boundaries are managed according to the terms of the 1964 Wilderness Act, which allows no permanent structures or motorized traffic on lands designated as wilderness. There are trails within the wild portion of the swamp, but the Youth Conservation Corps workers who maintain them use only muscle-powered tools. The going is necessarily slow, both for the maintenance crews and the hikers who use the trails, but wilderness is set aside for its own perpetuation, rather than for human convenience. Visitor access to this area is also restricted, primarily by limiting the number of parking spaces available at entry points.

If you set out early enough to get one of these spaces, or — better yet — if you visit the swamp on a weekday, you are in for a hiking experience for which no amount of exposure to the metropolitan area's other wild places can prepare you. There are great trees shrouding the banks of serpentine waterways, the surfaces of which might ripple with the movement of a spotted turtle or a water snake. Wood ducks live in the cavities of trees, and owls — screech, barn, barred, and great horned — sleep by day in the far upper branches. Bird life in the swamp is a volume in itself; over 200 species have been identified within the refuge since 1960. A *partial* list of those known to nest there might include green heron, least and American bittern, Canada goose, mallard and black duck, green-winged and blue-winged teal, red-shouldered hawk, American kestrel, king and Virginia rail, sora, common snipe, yellow-billed and black-billed cuckoo, five varieties of woodpecker and four of flycatcher, Eastern bluebird (the largest breeding bluebird population in New Jersey), scarlet tanager, indigo bunting, blue-winged warbler, and Louisiana waterthrush. Lest you spend all your time looking up, remember that this is the only location in New Jersey where the blue-spotted salamander lives. The adults of this species venture above ground only at the time of the first thaw, when they breed, but the juveniles can be seen in wooded areas from August to November.

Although much of the swamp wilderness resembles the setting of *The African Queen*, the first-time visitor might be surprised by the amount of dry, wooded upland and meadow within the refuge. This variety of terrain is reflected in the profusion of plant cultures that thrive here. The northern and southern botanical zones overlap in the swamp; there are oak, beech, mountain laurel, rhododendron, cattails, sassafras, pickerelweed, tupelo, blueberries, wild strawberries, and skunk cabbage. The swamp is a paradox: it is at once a place of deep silence and a cacophony of color, texture, and the music of birds.

There are mammals in the swamp, mostly ranging in size from shrews and voles to beavers (reintroduced in 1969) and fox — and bear tracks were seen on one occasion during the years since the refuge designation. But the animal which has gained the most public attention here is the whitetail deer. Deer hunting is allowed throughout rural New Jersey, but there is something

161

about the taking of these animals on land set aside as a refuge that rankles many preservationists, as well as anti-hunters who would as soon see the practice ended everywhere. The management of the refuge, however, has long been aware of the problems of disease and starvation within the swamp's deer herd. The reason is plain: in most years, there are too many deer for the carrying capacity of the land. In terms of available forage, the 13,000 acres that constitute the Great Swamp basin (of which the refuge makes up about half) can comfortably support about 600 deer in summer and 400 in winter. In order to keep the herd trimmed to these optimal numbers and prevent attrition due to malnutrition and disease, refuge managers decided, in the late 1960s, to allow a controlled hunt.

It wasn't that simple. Court action held up the hunt for years; now that it does take place (the refuge is closed to all but a computer-selected group of 600 permitees for 10 days during early December), participants are greeted at the entrance to the swamp by placard-bearing demonstrators who abhor the idea of the hunt. Although the demonstration now lasts only a few hours instead of the several days common in the early 1970s, it remains a pre-Christmas Jersey ritual: the hunt begins, and the hunters and anti-hunters show up. The deer wait in the interior, some marked for survival, and some for one sort of demise or the other.

PUBLIC TRANSIT: The Great Swamp lies in a portion of New Jersey served by very little in the way of mass transportation. An exception is the commuter rail network that originates at the Conrail (NJ Transit) terminal in Hoboken; these trains stop at communities such as Basking Ridge, Chatham, and Stirling, none of which, although they encircle the Great Swamp, are situated within a reasonable walking distance of its main entrances. Until such time as Conrail (NJ Transit) makes room for bicycles on its commuter trains (an idea that might well be worth a few letters),

the best bet for a carless swamp walker with a few dollars to spare would be a taxicab from one of the larger town stations on the outskirts of the refuge.

AUTOMOBILE: Take Interstate 80 to Interstate 287 south. Get off at exit 26A and follow signs for the refuge.

Refuge headquarters are open from 8 AM to 4:30 PM Monday through Friday; here you may obtain maps and copies of regulations for the area. As you approach the headquarters by car, remember that parking or stopping of vehicles is prohibited except at designated areas. This is the wildlife management section of the refuge, and animals — particularly the deer and geese you might see from the road at certain times — are more likely to be frightened or upset by people stopping or getting out of cars than by vehicles moving slowly down the road. Pleasant Plains Road is closed to traffic within the refuge between dusk and 8 AM, and even pedestrians are discouraged in these hours.

THE WALK: First, dress properly. Don't wear anything you wouldn't want to get wet. This doesn't mean that you're bound to be soaked; as was mentioned above, many areas are high and dry. But a swamp is a swamp, and once you are afoot in the wilderness area you will not want your movements checked by fear of getting wet feet. Canvas shoes are good, as are hip waders if you are really determined. Trails are blazed within the wilderness, but given the possibility of alterations and new additions, it would be imprudent to commit any routes to print. A visit to refuge headquarters will bring you up to date on the wilderness trail system, which includes 8½ miles of marked trails. Hiking is not permitted in that section of the refuge set aside for wildlife management.

There is a wildlife observation center near the border of the wilderness and wildlife management sectors within

GREAT SWAMP

Great Swamp. Facilities include a one-mile boardwalk loop. For further information on the Great Swamp National Wildlife Refuge, write headquarters at R.D. 1, Box 152, Pleasant Plains Road, Basking Ridge, New Jersey 07920.

18

VERDRIETEGE HOOK

Walking — majestic views of the Hudson River and surrounding highlands along a 6½-mile crest trail between Nyack and Haverhill, New York, with a water-level return route.

THIS IS A WALK ALONG the spine of Verdrietege Hook, a lofty and abrupt formation on the west bank of the Hudson River that separates the broad expanse of the Tappan Zee from Haverstraw Bay. "Verdrietege," in Dutch, may be roughly translated as "tedious," and so indeed was the sailing around the Hook when there was a stiff headwind to deal with. The walking here can also be a bit of work, as there are many ups and downs as you cross the summits of the hills known as the Seven Sisters, but it is never tedious. There are fine views of the Hudson and, along the crests when you reach the occasional clearing, expansive westward vistas of Rockland, Congers, and De Forest Lakes.

Dutch names for things, of course, are not at all uncommon in this part of the world — the salient natural feature of the place being the Tappan Zee, or "sea," itself. The west shore of the Hudson near what is now the New York-New Jersey boundary was settled in 1682 by a group of sixteen New York and New Jersey Dutch burghers and freed slaves who called themselves the Tappan patentees, after the name (its etymology is uncertain) of the territory immediately west of the Palisades, part of which is now the town of Tappan. The land they selected was purchased from the Indians for a sum of wampum, along with firearms, powder, lead, knives, tools, kettles, blankets, cloth-

ing, twenty gallons of rum, and four casks of beer. In the currency of the day, this no doubt amounted to a higher price than the $26 Peter Minuit is alleged to have paid for Manhattan Island.

As with the Minuit deal, the sellers were probably not even long-term inhabitants of the land the Dutch were buying. The Indians in the Nyack area had moved there from the vicinity of what is now Fort Hamilton, in Brooklyn, when the Dutch first came to Staten Island not many years before. In any event, we can see that the practice of buying land from the Indians for guns and booze was already established in the Hudson Valley of 300 years ago.

Verdrietege Hook is an eastern extension of the Ramapo Range, the chain of hills that rolls across the border country to the west. In geologic terms, it represents the point where the diabase sill of the Palisades Formation changes to a dike and curves inland to the Ramapo Front. A sill, in geologists' parlance, is a horizontal igneous intrusion *between* layers of pre-existing sedimentary rock, while a dike consists of the cooled and hardened aftermath of a vertical intrusion cutting *through* older rock layers. It all happened here 190 million years ago, as the red sandstone of the Newark Basin was shot through with molten rock and the raw material of the Palisades was formed (see Chapter 15).

As with the main formation of the Palisades to the south, these peculiarities of ancient rock formation are responsible for the dizzying cliffs and splendid views among the hills along the Hook, but they also attracted a vigorous nineteenth-century stone quarrying industry that threatened to flatten the majestic west bank of the river. If we are to believe early paintings of the region, some of the cliffs actually extended beyond the perpendicular and beetled out over the river. Certainly nothing like this exists today. The Palisade-like buttresses of Verdrietege Hook were dynamited mercilessly right on into the 1890s, and were only protected by the expansion of Palisades Interstate Park in the years 1906 through 1915. (The surrounding territory is

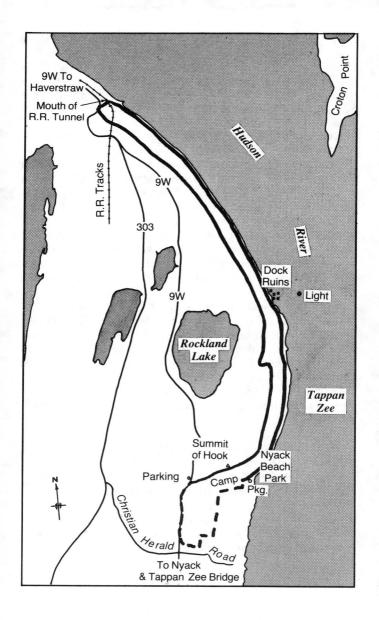

9W To
Haverstraw

Mouth of
R.R. Tunnel

R.R. Tracks

9W

303

9W

Hudson

Croton Point

River

Dock
Ruins

Light

*Rockland
Lake*

*Tappan
Zee*

Summit
of Hook

Parking

Camp
Pkg.

Nyack
Beach
Park

N

Christian Herald

Road

To Nyack
& Tappan Zee Bridge

called Hook Mountain State Park today.) So the profile of this terrain has been softened somewhat, and while we enjoy today's walks and views it's hard not to imagine how the Hook might have looked if crushed stone hadn't been such a hot item in old New York.

Another kind of quarrying went on in this area until the 1920s — the quarrying of a renewable resource eventually made obsolete by the freon coils in our refrigerators. Ice was cut from the surface of Rockland Lake and stored in huge adjacent icehouses from 1831 to 1924. The logistics of shipping the product involved a railway leading from the lake over the crest of the Hook to the Hudson, where at one time a fleet of 13 steamboats and 80 barges were loaded for the trip downriver to New York. In the city, Rockland Lake ice commanded top prices. The Astor House, one of New York's poshest nineteenth-century hostelries, had already contracted for delivery a year before it opened.

Very little remains to remind us of the great ice operation. The last of the icehouses near the lake burned in 1926, with the insulating sawdust in the ruins smoldering for two years afterwards. (The lake and its surroundings are now a state park.) On the Hudson side, we can still see the pilings of the vanished docks where barges were loaded with ice. As you head south on the return leg of this walk, look for these skeletal ruins in the vicinity of the little lighthouse that marks the eastern extreme of the Hook.

PUBLIC TRANSIT: Red and Tan Lines operates buses between New York City and the Nyack-Haverstraw area along Route 9W. Early in the day, they originate at the Port Authority Bus Terminal near the Manhattan end of the George Washington Bridge; later buses leave the Port Authority terminal in midtown. Buses will discharge passengers at any point along Route 9W; for details on where to get off the bus, see the instructions for automobile travel

*below. Call Red and Tan Lines for bus information at
212-279-6526.*

*AUTOMOBILE: From New York, take the Henry Hudson
Parkway north to the Tappan Zee Bridge. Cross the bridge
and get onto Route 9W north. Take 9W through the town of
Nyack and watch for Christian Herald Road. Park at a wide
spot on the left shoulder just 0.7 miles past Christian
Herald Road.*

*Note: Although it is perfectly feasible to begin and end
this walk at the parking spot indicated above, it is recommended that you spot a second car at the main parking lot at
Nyack Beach Park, immediately north of the town, at the
end of Broadway. Otherwise, it will be necessary to backtrack on suburban streets for over a mile in order to cross
the southern edge of the ridge and get back to Route 9W,
where a right turn and uphill walk will remain before you
get to your car. Nyack Beach Park is at the end of the
river-shore path that constitutes the return leg of the walk.*

*It is possible, of course, to spot a car in Haverstraw, 2
miles north of the northern extreme of the walking route
described here. Likewise, walkers returning to New York
via Red and Tan bus can board on Route 9W at the Haverstraw end of the walk and skip the return trip. Make sure of
your bus schedule, and avoid getting stranded. If you can,
though, make the entire loop on foot. The return leg is level
and pleasant and affords fine river views.*

*THE WALK: From the turnout where you parked or got off
the bus, backtrack a short distance, walking carefully on
the other side of the road. Look for a mailbox and a "No
Trespassing" sign. Head away from the road and down the
slope a short distance from this point (the sign applies to the
gravel path leading uphill) and look for the blue blazes that
mark the trail. Turn left onto the trail.*

VERDRIETEGE HOOK

The first scenic vista appears after twenty minutes or so of uphill hiking. This is the summit of Verdrietege Hook, from which you can see the Tappan Zee and its bridge, with glimpses of New York City to the south. To the north is Haverstraw Bay and, on the opposite shore, Croton Point. Rockland Lake lies in the valley inland from the river, with one of the area's remaining quarries nearby.

From the top of the Hook, follow the blue blazes northwards. The walk is a succession of valleys and summits (these hills, remember, are called the "Seven Sisters"), with occasional broad views to the west. Toward the northern end of the outbound trip, past a paved park road and a tiny, iron-fenced old graveyard (right side of trail), Hudson River views open up as well.

After you have covered about 6½ miles, the blue blazes will lead you to Route 9W (Haverstraw is 2 miles north of here). Just to your right, at this point, you will see an abandoned concrete trestle, along with an overgrown gravel road. Loop down onto this road and follow it to a railroad track. (This is an active line, so use caution when crossing or walking near the track.) If you cross the track and walk south (right) toward the mouth of a tunnel, you will be able to slab down the short slope to the river-shore trail without much difficulty.

From here, it is roughly 5½ miles along the paved path to Nyack Beach Park. Don't take any of the branch trails leading uphill to your right; just continue along the shore and you'll reach the park. If you haven't spotted that second car here, walk out of the park entrance, take a left, then turn right at the next corner and walk past the summer camp. Turn left onto Midland Avenue after one block and continue past four of the blocks on your right. Turn right, then left, then right again and continue to 9W, where a right turn will take you to your car.

19

AUDUBON CENTER, GREENWICH, CONNECTICUT

Walking — up to 5 miles, depending on trails taken. Wildlife preserve and nature center owned and managed by the National Audubon Society, located on old farmland since returned to forest.

TWO RIDERS WERE APPROACHING. The gentleman wore a cap, tweeds, and heavy corduroy breeches; he handled his chestnut mare effortlessly enough to devote all attention to his young woman pupil, who rode just in front of him. She wore a black riding cap, twill trousers, and a down vest over a lambswool turtleneck. Her attention was divided between immediate control of the animal and the firm, economical instructions of her teacher. Between admonitions regarding the approach to a stile, he noticed the walker; without changing tone, he said "Good morning, good morning." His accent was public school British. "Looks like a bit of snow, eh?" The woman neared the stile, horseflesh rippling beneath her, and the instructor turned to make his appraisal. The walker moved along, turning back to watch the jump, as the skies lowered over Greenwich.

This little vignette is apropos of the fact that it is quite easy to wander beyond the boundaries of the Audubon Center in Greenwich, Connecticut, and to be reminded that you are in the heart of what could only be called an American shire. It is fortunate, for those of us who do not live or take riding lessons there, that Audubon has custody of a lovely 477-acre corner of it.

The land occupied by the Audubon Center in Greenwich has had a history representative of nearly all of the northeastern forest — or at least of those parts of it which have never been urbanized. It has, in succession, been dense woods, small subsistence farms, market farms, an estate, and — here is where good fortune intervenes and makes this story atypical — a preserve for public enjoyment. The alternative, throughout much of Westchester and southwestern Connecticut, has been subdivision and suburban development, with the density of people and houses largely determined by the simple fact of median income. Here in Greenwich, trees, birds, and small mammals generally share in the comfort of their human neighbors.

Of course the Indians were here first. Archaeologists have turned up campfire remains which date to 1200 A.D., and perhaps earlier. The tribe that occupied the tiny Connecticut "panhandle" and adjacent areas of Westchester was a branch of the Wappinger Confederacy known as the Siwanoy. They were primarily engaged in fishing and farming by the time the first white settlers arrived, although their hunting needs were served, as among Indians elsewhere in the northeast, by a practice that belied the popular notion that an uninterrupted climax forest once stretched from Maine to Chicago. The Indians set fire to the forest with considerable regularity, their object being the creation of openings in which deer, rabbit, and upland birds could browse for food. Breaks in the forest were also caused by lightning fires and by beavers, whose ponds inundated low-lying stands of trees, then receded to leave new ground on which thicket could take hold. Ironically, there is some danger in our modern understanding of these natural means of interfering with forest growth. Opponents of strict wilderness preservation point to the advantages offered certain species of wildlife by timber cutting, and argue that the overmature climax stands that characterize eastern wilderness are an invitation to its very destruction by fire. It should be asserted, though, that we are in no danger of denuding too few acres of trees (compare our popula-

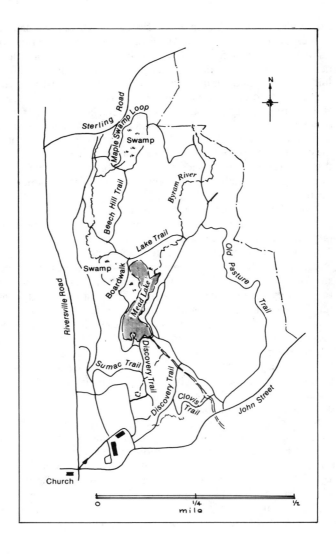

tion with that of the Indians), that fire can be a beneficial natural process, and that the popularity of some species as game is not in itself an argument for their over-proliferation. There are more deer in this country today than there were when Europeans first laid eyes on it, and our land use habits are the main reason why.

Englishmen came to Greenwich in 1640. The biblical Esau sold his birthright for a mess of potage; for a large chunk of their ancestral lands, the Siwanoys received eleven coats. History does not record which eleven Indians got to wear the coats, or if they were shared, but we do know that the property fetched by this apparel was soon divided among 22 farming families. This number grew to include the colonial proprietors of the farms that occupied the current Audubon holdings.

Now the real clearing of the land commenced. The average primeval acre, in this part of the country, supported about 80 large trees. At the rate of about one acre per man-year of work, the woods were turned into pasture and cropland. There were exceptions — hollows and steep ridges — but the steady expansion of agriculture in the valleys north of New York resulted in a remarkably clean-shaven landscape. The mid-nineteenth century was the highwater mark for farming in this area. At that time, between two-thirds and three-quarters of the terrain was clear of trees. It is said that in parts of nearby Westchester, residents could take to high ground with spyglasses and watch the construction of buildings in lower Manhattan, some 40 miles distant. They could no doubt watch their neighbors in Greenwich and be watched as well, but there was too much work to be done then to take time out for such foolishness.

It is worth noting that the landholdings farmed in New York and New England during the eighteenth and early nineteenth centuries were quite small by modern standards. The Mead farm, which makes up the heart of today's Audubon Center, totalled only 38 acres when it was purchased by Benjamin Mead, Sr. in 1743. It had grown to 138 acres by 1746, but the near-equal division of the land among four of Benjamin's sons left a cluster of small farms in its place. The largest of these belonged to Zebediah Mead, who built the Georgian farmhouse which still stands at the center. At his death in 1789 he owned only 90 acres. Nearly 100 years later, his heir Henry Mead died leaving somewhat less than that. The economics of modern farming, which dictate the incorporation of more and more land into an individual enterprise if a profit is to be realized, had not yet taken hold in the days when Westchester and Greenwich supplied potatoes, hay, and apples to New York City.

By the time of Henry Mead's death, farming days were nearing their close in this part of the northeast. Fields went fallow, and trees began to grow undisturbed once more. But the diminished need for cropland was not the only reason for the reappearance of the forest. The gradual replacement of wood with coal as a heating fuel had a lot to do with it, as did the later revolution in transportation brought about by the automobile. When horses were the primary mode of travel, it was necessary to keep them in pasture. After the passing of Dobbin, his fields went into second growth and ultimately to timber. (Cars, we have now learned, have their own open-space requirements. Unfortunately, the hard black fields they prefer will take a lot longer to turn fallow when the time comes.)

Consolidation of the small farms into non-agricultural holdings began around the end of the 1800s. The Meads' property, along with that of other nearby farming families, was purchased between 1905 and 1916 by William T. Carrington. After he died, in 1934, his wife put a covenant on the deed requiring that the estate's purchasers use the land only for residential purposes. Whether this reflected a dim view of agriculture or a desire to exclude commerce and industry is not known, but the new owners, H. Hall and Eleanor Clovis, engaged in none of these things. And in 1942, the Clovis family donated their 281 acres to the National Audubon Society for scientific and educational use. In that year, Audubon officially opened the center. Over three centuries, this southwesternmost corner of New England has come full cycle, forest to forest, with evidence of each phase of its usefulness scattered along its trails. There is an old mill pond, its sawmill and waterwheel now gone; a spring house and a root cellar; an old apple orchard; the Mead house and its outbuildings; broken remains of stone walls that once divided field and pasture; and buried artifacts of both Indians and settlers that occasionally come to light. There are more than just artifacts: between the Mead and Clovis houses lie the unmarked graves of British soldiers, who fought in the Revolutionary War raids staged throughout this area under the command of Lieutenant Colonel Banastre Tarleton. Tarleton, whose nickname was "the Green Dragoon," was a dashing rake whose notoriety as a womanizer rivalled his reputation as a soldier. The men of his command who fell here were returning from a raid when they were ambushed by farmers from nearby Round Hill.

The National Audubon Society administers the Greenwich Center as both a wildlife preserve and teaching resource, roles for which its botanical and topographical variety make it uniquely suited. Included within the center's property are swamp, upland forest, river, pond, and second-growth environments (a bayberry field and nannyberry thicket help make up the latter); also, hundreds of berry-producing trees have been planted to offer food for migratory and year-round bird species. Along the shore of Mead Lake are bird blinds, keys to which are available at the administration building. An outdoor classroom and interpretive center are located near the entrance, where you will find a comprehensive book shop typical of those found at Audubon facilities. The buildings that house the center's staff are unobtrusive and wisely clustered near the beginning of the trail system, leaving the rest of the preserve wild and free of man-made alterations — with the quite permissible exceptions of the trails themselves and Mead Lake.

The Audubon Center in Greenwich, 613 Riversdale Road, Greenwich, Connecticut 06830 is open Tuesday through Sunday from 9 AM to 5 PM. Admission is $1.00. For information regarding educational programs, call 203-869-5272.

AUDUBON CENTER (Greenwich, CT)

PUBLIC TRANSIT: Unfortunately, the center is not served by any direct — or even acceptably indirect — means of public transit.

AUTOMOBILE: Take the Hutchinson River Parkway to the Merritt Parkway. Get off at exit 28, which is the first exit after the toll booths at the Connecticut border. (Don't confuse this with exit 28 on the Hutchinson in New York state.) Drive north (left) approximately 1½ miles on Round Hill Road, turning left onto John Street at the white church. After another 1½ miles, you will see another white church on your left. Turn sharply right here into the Audubon Center entrance.

THE WALK: There are at least five miles of trails within the Audubon Center property. Depending upon age and ambition, it is possible either to confine your walks to within a half mile or so of the entrance or to range farther, past the Byram River and Mead Lake, to the northern reaches of the preserve. Maps available at the interpretive building show the overall trail network and details of the shorter Discovery, Clovis, and Sumac Trails. The Lake Trail follows the west shore of Mead Lake, partly via boardwalk through a swamp, and is especially recommended for birders. North of Mead Lake, the Beech Hill Trail connects with the Maple Swamp route, which affords a close-up look at a swamp environment. Return to the entrance via the Old Pasture Trail and take note of the hardwood species, particularly oak and maple, which came to dominate this former open grazing land after its abandonment. The Old Pasture Trail, incidentally, is open to equestrian traffic over most of its length; you might exchange pleasantries here with some of the shire-folk.

20

MANHATTAN: THE GHOST OF A COUNTRY WALK

Walking — 6 miles.

THIS IS A WALK to the outskirts of a little town whose crooked streets, steep-gabled buildings, and thicketed environs exist only in distant memory. It is simple enough to put this memory into words, but to translate it into even the most fleeting picture in the mind's eye requires considerable imagination. Give it a try. The walk starts at Battery Park.

Just across State Street from the Battery is Bowling Green, bounded on the south by the Beaux Arts facade of the old U.S. Customs House. But this building is "old" only in the sense that it is no longer used for its original purpose; its 1907 construction makes it a rank upstart compared with the fort of New Amsterdam, which stood here early in the seventeenth century as protection for a small band of Dutch traders and colonial officials who had come to see if any money could be made at the southern tip of Manhattan Island. One of the men who held sway here — Peter Minuit — is famous for his $24 Manhattan land deal, and his successor — Peter Stuyvesant — for his bluster and paternal concern for the colony. Among the many things Stuyvesant had little tolerance for was urban congestion, which in his day meant the cramped quarters of the governor's residence inside Fort Amsterdam. So he moved to a house in the country, at the present corner of Whitehall and State Streets. This is somewhat to the south of what is believed to be the fort site; if our estimations are correct, this would make Peter Stuy-

vesant not only the first but very likely the last person to head in that direction on Manhattan in search of bucolic pleasures.

The countryside beyond Fort Amsterdam was a welcoming and abundant place, if we are to believe the early accounts. In 1654, Nicasius de Sille wrote to a friend in the Hague about his island home: "Oysters we pick up before our fort . . . some so large they must be cut in two or three pieces." The undergrowth, claimed de Sille, consisted mostly of strawberries, catnip, and blackberries. Game also abounded — turkeys, venison, partridge, geese, and bear. For a while, Governor Stuyvesant must have lived the ideal commuter's life: a short walk to work, and all nature in his backyard.

But Stuyvesant soon had to range farther and farther in his peregrinations, if he was to put the noise of the growing town behind him. Walk up Whitehall to Pearl Street, and turn right. Now you are following the eastern shore of New Amsterdam; there were no Water or Front Streets, no South Street with its seaport. Stuyvesant could follow Pearl until he reached a wooden palisade, a wall, which he had ordered built in case the British or Indians decided to attack. But when the British did come, with their ultimatum of surrender, they came by sea. The town which they took, in 1664, had hardly grown beyond the wooden wall, by now standing long enough to be commemorated in the name of the street which took its place. In those years, Peter Stuyvesant made regular trips beyond this token barrier, to a farm he had established along the East River. The route he took acquired the name "Bouwerie," a Dutch word of the day for small agricultural landholdings.

Along the way, past the point where the landmass of Manhattan begins to bulge eastward, Stuyvesant, and those who followed his course for nearly a century and a half, could look to their left and see a small body of water called Collect Pond. In the days of New Amsterdam, the Collect was fit for fishing, swimming, and drinking, but as the city approached, its waters grew more and more foul. During the first decade of the 1800s it

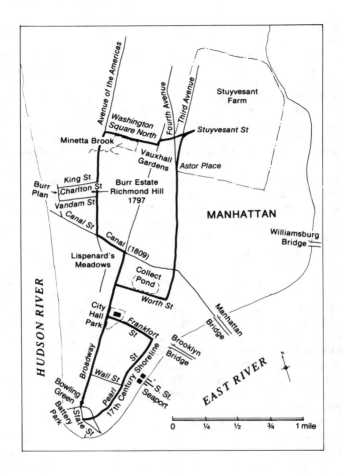

was filled in. The pond's south bank roughly corresponded to present-day Worth Street, just north of Foley Square.

When Stuyvesant was governor, life was too hard for anyone to devote good pasture to anything so frivolous as growing flowers. But by the middle of the eighteenth century, New Yorkers could afford such luxuries, and a Swiss immigrant named Jacob Sperry established his gardens and hothouses near the southwestern corner of the old Stuyvesant holdings, where Bond, Great Jones, and West 4th Streets are today. After 1804, what had been the source for the bouquets and boutonnieres of old New York changed hands, and became known as Vauxhall Gardens. How to describe Vauxhall? There is nothing like it today — tables for sherbets and wine set along paths winding through groves of trees and beds of flowers; fireworks; a band. The fun lasted for a quarter-century before the city, having breached Houston Street, swallowed the Gardens whole.

Old Stuyvesant's descendants saw the juggernaut approaching and made moves to profit from its advance. In 1789, Petrus Stuyvesant mapped out a street grid on the farm and even started to put up houses. But twenty years later, his layout, which ran due east and west, was found to conflict with the city's master plan, in which the cross streets were to be set instead at 90 degree angles to the northern and southern tips of the island. One of Stuyvesant's streets remained and bears the family name today. It angles through the block otherwise defined by Second and Third Avenues and East 9th and 10th Streets. Numbers 21 and 44 on this stubborn thoroughfare were once Stuyvesant family homes.

West of what we now call the East Village lies "the Village" — Greenwich Village itself. Appropriate though it might have been, the name does not derive from the community spirit evinced here during our time. It was called Greenwich Village because it *was* a village, situated well beyond the outskirts of New York. In the eighteenth century, Manhattanites from below Wall Street kept summer houses here, and even less wealthy individuals fled north to the secluded village during summer yellow fever epidemics. Around the 1820s, higher-density development began north of Houston Street. The 1830s Greek Revival row houses on Washington Square North are among the first built after city and village met. It is a house like one of these that forms the setting for Henry James's *Washington Square*.

Long before those brick homes and iron railings came to face the square, even before it served as a graveyard for the indigent and site for public executions, that patch of land now given to buskers and checker players was a swamp. No remnant of its watery past survives — at least not above ground — but Minetta Street and Minetta Lane, just southwest of Washington Square, keep alive the name of the brook that flowed through here over two hundred years ago, and for countless quiet centuries before that. Like so many of the natural waterways that coursed through Manhattan, Minetta Brook was buried and forgotten; but like some, it has occasionally come back to haunt the basements of modern-day householders.

South of Houston Street, three streets extend from the Avenue of the Americas. These are King, Charlton, and Vandam streets, planned in 1797 by the owner of a rambling hilltop mansion that stood near here. Don't look for either hill or mansion; they were removed in the first decade of the nineteenth century. The gentleman who drafted the street plan that replaced them had also moved from the area, his public esteem ruined by the outcome of a duel. His name was Aaron Burr.

Canal Street runs a few blocks to the south. The neighborhood that begins here today is called Tribeca, for *Tri*angle *be*low *Ca*nal, but in the 1700s much of it was known as Lispenard's Meadows. The canal was built in 1809, about the time that Collect Pond was being filled, and its purpose was to drain the spongy meadows. The city's expansion had been blocked by the marshes that stretched virtually from river to river in this part of Manhattan; in fact, high tides would sometimes even flood clear across these lowlands, separating the wild and settled parts of the island. The new canal helped solve the problem, but it too soon disappeared. Why have thoroughfares on either side of the canal, when it could be covered over and made into a single street? That accomplished, why not use it as a sewer? Points taken, job done.

South of the old meadows, past the place where a 50-foot hill once barred Broadway from reaching above Duane Street, lies City Hall Park and, just beyond, blocks in which the buildings rise higher. The effect is that of a rough parabolic gap between these towers and their midtown counterparts, but geology rather than skyline symmetry is the reason behind this arrangement. The schist formation that anchors all high-rise construction in Manhattan disappears deep beneath the surface at Washington Square, and does not come within reasonable reach of excavators until the vicinity of Chambers Street. From there it rises steadily, until less than 40 feet separate it from ground level at Broadway and Wall Street. This part of town, then, has a secure foundation, in the physical if not always in the figurative sense.

At this wall, we leave the countryside behind, re-entering New Amsterdam and walking the last blocks to Bowling Green and the Battery. There the fort, town, and city are left behind too; there the Hudson River, no longer hemmed by piers and Palisades, and the East River, washing down its short way from Long Island Sound, flow together into the Lower Bay, pour through the Narrows, and lead, like Conrad's Thames, to the uttermost ends of the earth.

THE WALK: Start at the foot of Pearl Street, which begins at Battery Park two blocks south of Bowling Green. Walk north on Pearl, past Wall Street and the restored blocks near the South Street Seaport. When you reach the approaches to the Brooklyn Bridge, turn left and walk along Frankfort Street to reach City Hall Park. (City Hall, which is open to visitors, is well worth a stop.) From City Hall, walk north (right) along Broadway to Worth Street, then turn right. This part of Worth Street roughly occupies the site of the south bank of Collect Pond. At Chatham Square, where Worth Street ends, turn north onto the Bowery. Walk

up the Bowery to the beginning of Fourth Avenue, at Astor
Place. (Beautiful or debased, no part of this city deserves to
be ignored. But if you haven't got a pocketful of spare
change, or have already seen what a surfeit of muscatel can
do, you can skip this section of Peter Stuyvesant's walk by
taking the subway north from City Hall to Astor Place.)
Turn right on Astor Place, then head north for one block on
Third Avenue and turn right onto East 9th Street and
Stuyvesant Street, where you can see Nos. 21 and 44.
Backtrack on Astor Place to Broadway, turn left, and walk
one block to Waverly Place. Turn right onto Waverly Place
and follow it past the point where it becomes Washington
Square North, with the park on your left and the row houses
on your right. After the park this street again becomes
Waverly Place; follow it until you reach the Avenue of the
Americas and turn left. Minetta Lane is four blocks south on
your left. Continue down the Avenue of the Americas to
Canal Street, turn left, and, counting five of the blocks on
your left, walk to Broadway. Turn right onto Broadway,
along which you can continue, if you wish, directly back to
the Battery.